FIRST CLASS
FATHERHOOD

ALEC LACE

FIRST CLASS FATHERHOOD

Advice & Wisdom from High-Profile Dads

HARPER HORIZON

Published by Harper Horizon, an imprint of HarperCollins Focus LLC.

Book design by Aubrey Khan, Neuwirth & Associates.

Any internet addresses, phone numbers, or company or product information printed in this book are offered as a resource and are not intended in any way to be or to imply an endorsement by Harper Horizon, nor does Harper Horizon vouch for the existence, content, or services of these sites, phone numbers, companies, or products beyond the life of this book.

ISBN 978-0-7852-4104-1 (eBook)
ISBN 978-0-7852-4103-4 (HC)

Library of Congress Control Number: 2021944108

Printed in the United States of America
22 23 24 25 26   LSC   10 9 8 7 6 5 4 3 2 1

TO JESSICA. I LOVE YOU.

Are you waiting for your tires?

TO CHRIS, LOGAN, AIDEN, & EMILY.

You make me feel like a First Class Father every day.

As a dad, everything is going to change.

It's going to be exhausting, it's going to be challenging, it's going to sometimes seem impossible, but it's all worth it.

—TONY HAWK

Contents

Foreword

THOUSANDS OF HOURS of video footage of you being a dad can be eye-opening and, at times, cringeworthy, but it does force you to take an honest look at yourself and help you become a better father. *Little People, Big World* has provided me this opportunity.

Becoming a father was a radical change for me. I went from being super focused on my career to becoming the custodian of four precious lives. The responsibility was stunning. We had our twins first and one of them is a little person, like me and my ex-wife, Amy, who both have dwarfism, and one of them is average size, so we had our hands full. Having children revolutionized our perspective and our life, and it continues to do so to this day.

At times along my fatherhood journey, I thought I was being a great father because I was home and present. However, sometimes I was chasing my own vision for my kids' lives. For instance, three of my kids loved building forts, but my youngest one didn't. I pushed him on that for a few years and also tried to get him into wrestling, which I did as a kid. It can be difficult to know when to pivot and focus on children's unique interests, and I didn't always make those turns soon enough, because I was trying to influence them in a certain direction. Now, as a grandfather, I'm committed to understanding what they like.

If I had to pick one hero in my life, it would be my father. He was a huge presence in my life. We always ate dinner together as a family and prayed at the table together as a family. He shared some of the best wisdom with me, not just from the Bible but also about having confidence in myself and knowing I could be anything I wanted to be. He instilled in me a sense of self-worth and respect, and was an inspirational figure to me.

I don't expect my legacy as a dad to be that I was a perfect father. But I do want my kids and grandkids to look back and remember that I was always there—that we could sit down and have a conversation about anything, and that I would listen.

I've had the pleasure of getting to know Alec Lace well over the last few years and have enjoyed his company at the farm. I respect guys like Alec, who work multiple jobs while raising four kids and chasing a vision to promote fatherhood with his podcast, *First Class Fatherhood*. I'm amazed by what he does, and he inspires me.

Alec has hosted some of the most incredible fathers in the world on his podcast. My favorite part of the interviews, which I always anticipate, is when he asks his guests what advice they have for new or soon-to-be dads. His podcast and this book, both of which I'm honored to have been a part of, provide invaluable wisdom for dads—especially new dads.

As we look around our country right now, things seem chaotic. I truly believe, as I know Alec does, that if we could get our families back to the dinner table, praying together, this would create a ripple effect that would fundamentally improve our society. There is no rule book for fatherhood, and you'll often question yourself and your decisions as a dad. But having a toolbox full of advice and wisdom, captured by Alec in *First Class Fatherhood*, can be a guiding light on your fatherhood journey.

—MATT ROLOFF

Introduction

"**I**'M PREGNANT!"

The first time you hear your partner speak these words, the best chapter of your life is about to begin. Unfortunately, in part because of Hollywood and pop culture, many men feel that becoming a dad is something to avoid or fear and not something to aspire to or embrace. Many men are taught to believe having a wife and kids is a "ball and chain" that will prevent them from pursuing their dreams and hold them back from living a fulfilling life. And many messages from our culture tell us that true happiness can and will be found in material things.

As a part-time Uber driver, I saw this on the faces of the young men I drove around on the weekends. When I'd tell them I have four children, they'd look at me as if I had four heads. They'd rattle off the reasons they didn't have kids and why they weren't sure they ever wanted them. These experiences set me on a mission to change this negative perception of fatherhood and family life.

In January 2018, I was helping my kids try to start a YouTube channel. I was filming my daughter open packages of toys, because for some reason, videos of what's called "unboxing" seem to be popular. I explained to my kids that a lot of work goes into a successful channel—that it's more than turning on the camera and fooling around. I quickly discovered many skill sets are involved in making YouTube videos. While doing my research for how to create a channel and edit videos, I stumbled upon the new and fast-growing platform of podcasting.

To me, the most intriguing part of podcasting was that it was audio only and thus eliminated the need for shooting and editing videos. I borrowed some library books, and I was sold on the idea of starting a podcast—one that would give me the opportunity to spread my positive message about fatherhood, and to show my kids the amount of hard work that goes into making your own show. The first thing I needed was a name for the podcast.

I am the seventh and youngest child of a blended family. My father was fifty years old when I was born in 1980, and my mother was forty-two. At that time, my dad was selling cars on Jerome Avenue in the Bronx, New York. But back in 1955, he'd been a stand-in singer for Eddie Fisher during the days of the musical variety television series *Coke Time with Eddie Fisher*. At a young age I became a huge fan of the classic, old-school movies and TV shows. The Three Stooges, the Marx Brothers, James Cagney, Humphrey Bogart, and Edward G. Robinson, among others, were my favorites.

As I thought about a name for my podcast, I recalled a movie I'd seen several times, which featured Humphrey Bogart and Edward G. Robinson, *Brother Orchid*. In the film, Robinson plays a gangster and crime boss who's on a mission to acquire "class" by traveling the world and buying fancy material things. When he returns from a trip to Europe, one of his gang members, played by Humphrey Bogart, has taken control. Bogart decides to have Robinson whacked to get him out of the way. Hit men shoot Robinson several times, but he escapes. A monastery takes him in and nurses him back to health. Robinson becomes a novice member of the monks, to hide out and lay low for a while.

After spending time with the monks and observing them perform acts of service for the community without compensation and live a simple, quiet life, he feels that they're the biggest suckers in the world. He eventually returns to a life of crime and seeks vengeance on Bogart. At the end of the movie, however, he returns to the monastery and delivers a powerful monologue explaining how all his life he'd been a guy in search of class, and that he believed class came from nice clothes, expensive jewelry, and high society. He said he'd traveled the world and discovered one thing: the brothers at the monastery were the ones with the real class.

Another influence on my life was horse racing. I grew up frequenting OTB (Off Track Betting) in New York City and the Meadowlands Racetrack in New Jersey. I knew how to read the *Racing Form* before I ever read a book. One of the most important things to focus on when trying to handicap a horse race is the class of the horse. Horses can move up in class during their career. Class is made up of several characteristics, and many trainers will tell you that the fastest horse won't necessarily win the race—the horse with the most class will.

In horse racing, class is the ability of the horse to overcome any obstacle or challenge it faces during the race. Even though the horse is running out of gas, it doesn't show it. Even though the horse would love to quit, it never does. As the horses come down the home stretch, class determines the winner.

When you become a father, you are moving up in class. You may have no idea what you're doing. You'll get tired from all the sleepless nights, and the days may start to blend together. You may doubt yourself and question whether you can raise a child. But no matter how exhausted you get, you'll never quit because by becoming a dad, you have moved up in class. You have entered a class that has existed since the dawn of man and has an innate instinct to know what to do.

I decided to combine these two concepts and call my podcast *First Class Fatherhood*. Fatherhood is more than a finite thing. It is a happening. It connects us all. You will have struggles along this journey called fatherhood. Have faith in yourself and know that you can do it. There are over a billion dads on the planet, but there is only one you. No dad on Earth will have the same exact experience as you, yet we're all the same. We are not babysitters—we are fathers. And we're not just fathers—we're first class fathers.

Perspective

I **F YOU'VE EVER** flown on a plane, you know that before the flight takes off, the crew takes you through a preflight safety demonstration. They explain that should the cabin pressurization systems fail and the cabin loses pressure, compartments containing oxygen masks will open and one will drop in front of you. The crew then tells you, if you have children on board, to put your mask on first and then help your child. The reason is because if you're struggling to put the mask on your child and pass out, you're now useless to your child.

This concept may be difficult for new dads to grasp because of the paradigm shift that occurs in your world once you have a child. As fathers, we're all seeking the same thing—we want our children to feel safe, happy, and loved. We don't want to see them injured, depressed, or scared. When we put ourselves and our needs on the back burner to meet the needs of our new baby, it becomes easy to forget that self-care is important. I think this point is significant to keep in mind as we begin to explore how becoming a dad changes our perspective on life.

A Navy SEAL saying states, "Get comfortable being uncomfortable." While becoming a dad is natural, you will be put in some very uncomfortable situations. From your first diaper change to thawing out breast milk, embracing these moments will accelerate your fatherhood experience and help you grow in ways you never thought possible.

When it rains, everyone understands what's happening. No matter what language you speak or what part of the world you're from, there's a universal understanding of what's happening. You recognize the experience. Similarly, if you're sitting in the stands of a high school football game and one of the kids gets seriously injured and is lying on the field in agony, and a father bolts off the bleachers and runs onto the field, it makes no difference what color he is, what religion he is, what political party he belongs to, or anything else of that nature. As a dad, you feel empathy. The non-dad in the stands may feel bad for the guy, but he won't feel the same empathy you do as a father. The perspective is different.

I remember seeing the movie *John Q* starring Denzel Washington, when it first came out in 2002, before I was a dad. The story centers on a father whose young son needs a lifesaving heart transplant. At the time I thought the movie was an okay tearjerker but not so great as far as Denzel movies are concerned. Years later, after having my first two children, I revisited the film when it aired on TV, and it was emotionally hard for me to get through it. I don't believe I've ever cried more during a movie than I did the second time I watched *John Q*. My perspective had changed. I could now empathize with Denzel's character and appreciate his performance.

For some dads, this perspective shift happens immediately, while for others it may take a while. Below, you will read the responses from some of the incredible men I have interviewed, as they answer the question "How did becoming a father change your perspective on life?"

Dan Abrams

ABC CHIEF LEGAL ANALYST,

NEW YORK TIMES BESTSELLING AUTHOR

I WAS AN OLDER DAD. I became a dad at forty-six. I was talking with my son the other day about the day he was born, and his mom talked about the fact that I cried. My son says, "But, Daddy, I've never seen you cry before!" And I told him yeah, but I had never had a baby boy before. So for me it was everything. It was that life-changing moment where everything that matters comes together. It was the most exciting day. I look at the pictures of those first few weeks, and it was just a great bonding time between me and my child. And I'd say to dads: if you get the opportunity to take some paternity time, take it if you can; if you can't, just remember how important those moments are. Because at every age, you look back and say, "I can't believe how fast this has gone." These are precious moments and the most important thing in our lives.

Now my son is a big soccer player. He is sort of obsessed with soccer, which is kind of a bummer for me because as a kid growing up, I played just about every sport except for soccer. I have old cards, hockey cards, basketball cards, and football and all of that. All my son wants to talk about is soccer and European soccer and I'm like, "I don't know anything about this!" so I'm trying to learn.

Jordan Belfort

THE WOLF OF WALL STREET

I WAS THIRTY-ONE WHEN I became a dad, and listen—at that time, I looked at my daughter as the only pure thing in my life pretty much. Everything I had at that time was based on money, even my marriage, it was all based on sort of . . . I wouldn't say just all greed but fueled by just a wild, over-the-top lifestyle. It all had been somewhat corruptive, and then my daughter came into the world, and she was this perfect little creature, and I think I directed a lot of my love and used her to maintain some sort of my sanity, as well, by projecting stuff onto her. Thankfully, she turned out amazing.

My kids now all see my life the way it is today, and they see the life that I've built over the last ten years. I think if I would not have done that, I don't think the movie *Wolf of Wall Street* would've been a very good thing for my kids to see. That's how their dad went down? But I think my kids, what they have seen is that the movie ended, and I ended up building a life even more amazing and totally pure this time, and I think they look at that as their dad is empowering, that their dad is this amazing comeback guy. The gift I gave my kids was being honest about the mistakes I've made and then also going out there and rebuilding my life in a far better fashion.

Jason Belmonte

WORLD CHAMPION TEN-PIN BOWLER

I THINK IT JUST OPENS your eyes a little bit into the bigger picture. I don't know if this is something that happens to everybody—I would like to hope so—but there is this moment where you notice that the world does not revolve around you. That there are others in it that are equally important as you in this world. When I got married, that certainly was one of the first moments that I realized this. Then having our first child was like, wow—not only does the world not now revolve around you, but this little person is the most important person in the entire world. So it was one of those moments where you're so amazed at how little you are compared to another person, when that other person is your child.

Then going from one to two children is a little more challenging. I feel like now, right at this very moment, when two of my children are grown and busy somewhere else and I have just one to watch, it's honestly like a holiday. It's so easy to do, and I wonder and think back to the days when my oldest was first born, why did I think this was so difficult? This is so easy now. I think when we had two and we were juggling two kids and keeping two kids happy—not that it was incredibly difficult, but it was a step up.

Now, with three, I feel like I'm way more relaxed as a dad in that regard. You know, I don't let every little bump and scratch cause me to go running with the medical kit if there's a graze on the knee. Now I'm more like, "Hey, you'll be fine—get up!" Because I'm a lot more relaxed as a dad, I think it allows me to be a bit freer and independently do things with the three individual children rather than feeling like I have to carry them all at the same time. I have no problem now saying, "No, Daddy's a little busy with your brother, and I'll come back in a minute." Where before when it was just the two of them, I'd always feel like I was trying to keep them together. Oh, this one wants you and that one wants you. I'll do everything I can right now for both of you so you're both happy, and I don't think that's the way it's supposed to go.

Drew Bledsoe

NFL VETERAN, WINERY ENTREPRENEUR

THE NUMBER ONE THING THAT I tell people is that I don't think I knew what it meant to be afraid until I became a dad. I've never been known for driving slow; I've always been kind of a fast driver. But when we were driving home from the hospital for the first time with our son Stew, all of a sudden, I'm driving fifty-five miles an hour in the slow lane on the freeway.

I think when you become a dad, everything else in your life moves down the list of importance immediately, and all of a sudden it takes over the number one spot in your life, and everything else is less important or in some cases more important—but only because it is important to that role as a dad.

John Brenkus

PRODUCER, DIRECTOR—*SPORT SCIENCE*

I WAS THIRTY-TWO OR THIRTY-THREE, and the way that I became a father was interesting. My wife and I had probably only been married for a year or so, and she was out of town. We had a little two-seater convertible, and I was on Main Street in Venice, and some dude was driving—he was on his cell phone, and I could tell he wasn't gonna stop. I thought to myself, *I'm gonna die.* He hit straight into me, spun me around—it was a horrible car crash. And the only thought that went through my mind was, I haven't had a child yet. That was the first thought in my mind: *Oh my God, I'm gonna die and I haven't had a kid yet.* I called my wife, and I said, "I was just in a really bad car accident. We're gonna have kids. Right now! I know we haven't been married long but there's no better time than right now." So that really sent us down the road, and we were incredibly blessed.

We first had our son and then we had our daughter a couple of years after, and we are grateful and thankful. I definitely suffered from being worried. Like, *Oh my God, how am I going to handle this?* I had my own production company, and for whatever reason we are always concerned about finances, and we think to ourselves, *How am I going to afford this? How am I going to do this? How am I going to be a dad and still have a job and be able to balance everything?*

There were two thoughts that went through my mind that did help me. One was, there are over seven-and-a-half billion people on the planet, and I can't possibly be the least qualified person. I may not be the most, but I can't be the least, and a lot of people have figured this out. Then I had another moment, when you bring home your first child from the hospital, it's that very surreal experience, where you shut the door behind you, and all of a sudden, it's me, my wife, and this human that's a couple of days old. And you're like, *What do I do? How am I going to handle this?*

Very early on my son was up crying, and I went down the hall and picked him up and was holding him. As I was raining down love on my son and telling him it's going to be okay, I could feel

God's love raining down on me at that exact moment, saying, "It's gonna be okay—you're gonna figure this out." It was a really distinctive, powerful moment for me. When you surrender to the natural course, when you surrender to the universe—whatever religion you are—things do work out. They just do. If you're putting one positive foot in front of the other, good things will happen.

Tim Brent

NHL VETERAN, REAL ESTATE DEVELOPER

GOSH, YOU KNOW, I WISH I did it earlier. I wish my kids could've been a part of my hockey career. I never even considered having a daughter. When my wife, Eva, called me and said it's a girl, if you should've seen the look on my face: I was so dumbfounded. But becoming a father absolutely changed me as a man, and I mean that in the best possible way. I've never cared for anything as much as I do my kids. It's just the best feeling in the world, coming home from work and having my daughter run over and hug my leg or wanna give me a smooch or whatever it is. I am completely wrapped around her little finger, and I won't make any excuses about it—I love every minute of it.

At bedtime she has to pet a few of her stuffed animals, and then we say a prayer. I put her down, and recently she's asked me to sing a lullaby to her, which is "Twinkle Twinkle Little Star." We are so blessed because she's been such a great sleeper. Since she's been eight weeks old, she's been sleeping through the night. I know that we are spoiled with that and will probably have to pay for that with our next one.

A. J. Buckley

ACTOR—*SEAL TEAM, CSI: NY*

I APOLOGIZED TO MY PARENTS, and understood why they were worried all the time, after I had kids. I was like, "I get it and I'm sorry." Because I used to always tell my mom to stop worrying and that I'm fine. But now that I'm a dad, I'm like freaking out because with all of the internet stuff—and I have a daughter!

But becoming a dad has changed my life for the better. It's given me more focus and more drive. It has settled me down in the sense of what time is. You know work is work and family time is family time. Prior to having kids, I was just like work, work, work, work, and if you didn't fit into the work schedule, then I couldn't ever see you, as far as relationships or whatever. With kids it's like, no, when it's actual family time, it becomes time to put the phone away, and it becomes designated family time. You have to really separate the two, work and family time. That's what you want to do because that's what you're working so hard for, it's so you can have great family time.

Brian Chontosh

UNITED STATES MARINE, SILVER STAR RECIPIENT

I WAS EITHER TWENTY OR TWENTY-ONE when my daughter was born. I was on deployment, serving as a young corporal. It was interesting because at that age, you know, our emotional development is still on its journey too—maybe it is our entire lives. I was raised in a family where my parents and all my uncles started their families very early, and it was a part of that generation or circle of family that was what you do: you got out of high school, and you go to college, or you go join the service, and then you start a family. I was kind of a product of that.

I fell in love with an Icelandic girl, and we had a daughter, and it was awesome; it was incredible. In the military, OPTEMPO (Operations Tempo) was a little crazy, especially the last fifteen or twenty years. OPTEMPO was exceptionally high, and it takes its toll on families—no excuses. Then when you're talking about a twenty-one-year-old with all of those responsibilities, plus the added responsibilities of fatherhood or parenthood, things can get very, very confusing quick. And without a super strong support structure, things can go awry fast too. That's just a lot of pressure for somebody who doesn't have a whole lot of life experience to draw from.

There are added pressures of being on deployment, but in the Marine Corps (I'm sure the other services had it too), we had an exceptionally strong rear echelon or remain-behind unit, family support structure in place when units go on deployment. I think in recent years, that support network that stays at home while units deploy has gotten better and stronger, because of all these combat deployments and the high OPTEMPO. So that's cool that there's a ton of resources pouring in to help families, and a lot of it especially for the young families.

I don't think I was a particularly good parent or family figure at any time during my career. I routinely put my career first, and I'm fortunate to have this awareness that it's not too late. It isn't until the last six to eight years that I realized I need to prioritize my family to a greater extent, and it's something that I think about often, and it drives who I am today as a dad.

Adam "Edge" Copeland

WWE SUPERSTAR

I RETIRED FROM PRO WRESTLING when I was thirty-seven. Then Beth Phoenix and I got together after I retired, because she was a former pro wrestler as well. I was forty by the time we had our first child and almost forty-three by the time we had our second. So I obviously started later, and I think emotionally and from a maturity standpoint, I had gotten all of the other stuff out of my system. I had gone for that career that I wanted, I got it, I did it, and I accomplished all of that. So it didn't feel like I was missing out on something—I was truly ready and prepared to focus on being a dad.

You know, growing up without a dad, I had my grandpa and some uncles, but I didn't have any cues to take from. I really just wanted to be a present father figure. I think the age really helped me with that and having gotten my ya-yas out with wrestling for twenty years. I felt like I did everything I wanted to do, so I can fully be a partner and be a dad.

In terms of concerns, one of my concerns was energy wise. I hit forty; I felt it. Am I going to have the energy to keep up with my kids? Am I going to be able to roll around on the floor with them? But they keep you young because you have to get up. You have to go, you have to move, and they keep you spry, I guess, for lack of a better term. It is such an amazing thing to watch the leaps and bounds that they make. I could be gone for a week or two, and when I get back, I'm like, "What just happened?" Thankfully I'm home 90 percent of the time, so I get to be there for a lot of it.

Andrew East

NFL VETERAN, YOUTUBER

FINDING OUT THAT YOU'RE PREGNANT for the first time is such a roller-coaster ride in and of itself. You're kind of scared at first, and you think, *Oh my gosh, I don't think I'm prepared*! You go from an almost denial version of it to getting excited. You start dreaming about what you should name the child; you start looking at baby clothes, and it's fun.

My wife, Shawn Johnson, was at that point when we found out it was a miscarriage. So to find out it was a miscarriage was very difficult for her, and I think a lot of times the woman feels like it's her fault. But it's not the woman's fault at all. Sometimes it doesn't work out, and that's okay. So, going into the second pregnancy, it was special because in some ways, it was a full-circle experience. I think we were hesitant to fully dive into the experience and the excitement phase because you don't know how it is going to end. All you can do is pray for the best.

I feel like when I was first married to Shawn, I kind of realized another level of love, where it's like you realize you need to be self-less. And there is something amazingly fulfilling about not just focusing on yourself but considering your wife. Having a child, I feel, is the next step in that, just because there are so many in-stances where you're challenged by "Oh my gosh, it's 2:00 a.m. and she's crying again. Can't my wife just take care of it this time?" But it's been a really fun role for me to step into, just trying to do as much as I can to help my wife out because we are both stressed, we are both tired, and we are both trying to figure it out. It's like this amazing project that my wife and I get to work on, and we are having a blast so far.

Nick Hardwick

NFL VETERAN

I BECAME A DAD AT THIRTY YEARS OLD. As a professional football player, it was a really wild experience to become a dad and then go out and try to play such a savage role. As the center of the football team, I was the tip of the spear, and being a dad really softens you. I think when you come into the National Football League you feel like—looking back on my career, I laugh at this—you feel like one of the toughest men on the planet, and you feel almost immortal, and you feel like this is never gonna end. A couple of injuries led me to understand that this career is going to end. But then, when we had our first child, it made me realize that not only is my career gonna end, but if there is a start to life, there is definitely gonna be a finish to life, so this life that I'm living is going to end at some point. That was the overwhelming experience of having a baby for the first time, thinking, *This started somewhere, and it's going to end somewhere, and you'd better make the most of it.*

We had our first child the night before a game against the Baltimore Ravens, and the next morning, before I left to go to the stadium, the doctor came in and said he was going to do our son's circumcision and asked if I would like to come watch. I thought, *Well this is going to be interesting. I'm not sure how this is going to affect me before the game, but I'm certainly not going to miss out on this opportunity.* So I went into the room and held my son and helped to calm him down.

After the circumcision, we brought him back to the room. I kissed my wife, Jamie, on the forehead and said, "Baby, I'll see you after the game." And I'm telling you, I played one of my best games that I've ever played against the Baltimore Ravens, hours after watching my firstborn be circumcised, and it was so surreal. It felt like the game was a breeze—it was fun, it was refreshing to be out there, there was no pressure, there was no stress. I was as relaxed as I had ever been in my career, and I played, if not my best game, close to the best game I could've played the day after our first child was born. It was unbelievable.

Mike Haynes

NFL HALL OF FAMER

IT CHANGED MY LIFE BECAUSE I realized a lot—not during the pregnancy, but once my first child was born—I realized what a miracle! What a responsibility to be a father. In some ways I started passing judgment on my own dad. I hate to say it, but my dad was kind of an absentee dad, and before I thought I kind of understood that. But after having my own family, I realized that maybe my dad could've been better and focused on us a little more.

It's a great responsibility that I love, and it also helped me understand how, as parents, we can shape our kids to think and be certain types of people, just by the experiences we share with them. I realized there are so many things we need to be educated on to be good parents. So being a father and having that experience has really given me an opportunity to see how people can be shaped, how communities can be shaped, and how we need to be aware of what's going on.

Tyler Hilton

COUNTRY SINGER, ACTOR—*ONE TREE HILL*

IT DIDN'T CHANGE MY PERSPECTIVE when my daughter
was born as much as when we found out that we were pregnant. I
always looked at fatherhood with so much respect and so much
nervousness. I've always thought in the back of my head, *When I'm
a dad, I'm gonna do this and that.* It's kind of been the most important thing I knew I was going to do in my life. I've kind of tripped
out on it my entire life, so the moment it was gonna happen was
always gonna be a huge deal for me. And kind of like a lot of other
things in my life, when the moment actually happened, it was a lot
less scary or life changing than I thought, because I had tripped out
on it so much beforehand.

So when we found out that we were pregnant, I went hard into
all the books. I was like, "This is it! This is go time. It's a green
light—it's Dad time!" I just got really into it, and the whole time I
just kept thinking, *How am I gonna tour?* But I've always been
thinking that in the back of my head. *At some point, I'm gonna
have a kid. How is this gonna work, this whole touring life, this musician life with a kid? How is being on set gonna work?* I talked with
different actors and musicians I knew on the road who had kids,
and I asked their advice because I always knew this was the end-
game. So when the kid came, there wasn't that big of a change. If
anything, I'm surprised how relaxed I am. I think it's because I
had been thinking about it so much. But I loved reading all the
books, I loved learning about what babies do, what infants do, and
all the nitty-gritty about it. The books were really helpful those
first two weeks. That was like hell week during high school football for me.

Mike Iaconelli

PROFESSIONAL FISHERMAN, BASSMASTER CHAMPION

WE HAD OUR FIRST DAUGHTER when I was in my midtwenties. I had just started my professional career in fishing. I would say it grounded me, which had a lot of positive effects. As a young man back then, there was a lot of anxiety in starting the sport and traveling so much. One of the things with professional fishing is there's so much travel, and I think having a child really grounded me in the fact that, no matter what happened to me in the professional realm, I knew I had a lot of responsibility on the fatherhood side. I also had a lot of love on that side, and that grounded me. You know, flash-forward twenty years—I don't know that I would have had the career I've had, the success I've had, and I don't know if I'd be the person I am if I hadn't had a child in my midtwenties. So it was great.

And another thing I can tell you is that with each child, I feel like I learned something. I've gotten a little better as time has gone on. But also, everyone is different. What worked for my first child, the same things don't necessarily work for my youngest one.

I can tell you that there are so many benefits of fishing with your kids. The big one is, fishing, to me, is one of the last great activities or sports that connects you and connects a child with nature. Being outside and being in nature, there's a beauty to it. Being outdoors and fishing teaches you so many great life lessons. It teaches kids things that are hard to learn in other parts of life. It teaches them patience. You have to learn patience to be a fisherman. It's a puzzle, so you have to learn putting pieces of the puzzle together. You have to learn how to read what's in front of you. You have to learn about the environment. You have to learn about weather. There are all these cool things that happen when you go fishing, and I think it's great, and it connects you with your children in a way you wouldn't believe. So it has been an interesting journey, and it's been awesome. I would never have done it another way.

Bill Klein

REALITY TV STAR—*THE LITTLE COUPLE*

I DON'T THINK I COULD'VE planned it better if I had every choice in front of me. When we first started off, Jennifer and I got engaged and we were immediately interested in adoption. We submitted our information to LPA, a community that supports people with skeletal dysplasia, or little people. We put our names on a list and kind of forgot about it for a while. We knew that it would be a while before our name was called.

Knowing Jennifer's petite stature might cause complications during pregnancy, we opted to try surrogacy. We went through the surrogacy process and successfully transferred embryos to our surrogate. Sadly, of the two most promising transfers, one resulted in a miscarriage and the other in what is called a chemical pregnancy. And then I guess destiny, God, put us in the right spot to receive William.

We received his profile from Rainbow Kids; and we fell in love immediately. We pursued him aggressively, addressed all of the paperwork, and before we knew it, we were on our way to China. A few short months passed by before we found ourselves on a trip to complete our family by going to Mumbai, India, to bring home our daughter, Zoey.

Having kids changed everything. I'm grateful for all of the decisions that led us to Will and Zoey. Without them, our home and our hearts wouldn't be the same.

Nick Mangold

NFL VETERAN, ENTREPRENEUR

I WAS TWENTY-SIX WHEN I became a dad for the first time. It was amazing, and the biggest thing that caught me was, you know, when we were coming out of the hospital after two or three days. We are walking out the front door, I go get the car, and we load him up in the car seat, and my wife and I both sit down and we're like, "So they're just letting us leave with him? There's no other, like, test that I have to do?" I had to do more tests to get my driver's license than I did for a human.

So it was life changing. It was neat seeing how my life was now taking care of a child, because we were married four or five years before we had children, so it was always my wife and me, and I always felt like I was taking care of her and I was responsible for her, but now to have a life in my hands who is just lying there, eating, sleeping, doing its business—it was crazy. It gave me so much more energy and so much more excitement that I get to do this for him.

I always compared the number of kids you have to defenses. When you have one, you're playing double-team, man. When you have two, it is man on man. When you have three, you're in a zone, so I figured when we had four, we're already in zone anyway. How hard can it be? It also happens that our fourth was the first one we had while I wasn't playing, so I was home a lot more, and that was a huge transition. It probably took about four months for me to get out of that newborn fog and realize that life still goes on, and I've got to figure out how working life with four kids instead of three kids is going to work. So going from three to four for me was huge.

We have two boys and two girls, and it's been neat seeing how similar and how different they are. I don't think we are doing anything different as parents, but it's just their own personalities.

Joel McHale

ACTOR, COMEDIAN—*THE SOUP*

IT CHANGES EVERYTHING. I want to meet the guy who was like, "Eh, it was fine—it was just a blip." It changes everything, because I think you figure out that you're really not that important. It's all about your children, not screwing them up, hopefully. It was just the greatest thing, and whenever I hear people go, "Oh man, you're in for it! You get that baby, man, you're just in baby jail for like a year, man!" I'm just like, this is the greatest thing, and I can't believe there is a human being that I love this much. I just could not stop holding him and hugging him; I couldn't believe it.

Now he's like 180 pounds, so it's very difficult to do that. I would say that both of those births, I was like, I can't believe how lucky I am. I just smother them with love. My goal is to raise good kids who become good people. If I can just raise kids who are good, I will be very happy.

Dakota Meyer

UNITED STATES MARINE, MEDAL OF HONOR RECIPIENT

IT CHANGED EVERYTHING. I think its equivalent to you looking at the world while standing on the ground to all of a sudden looking at the world from the space station. That is probably still an understatement of how much it changed my world. The number one thing is it taught me what love was, it taught me what true love was, it taught me what forgiveness was, it taught me what empathy was, and it taught me all of that. The other part of it is that it taught me to grow up and gave me a perspective of how to be a man.

And a lot of men, the divorced guys out there who are not really fathers. You know, they are doing the minimum. They are doing what society allows them to do instead of fighting to be a father. I'll tell you an example—the typical standard schedule for a father, because society has set this standard, which is so messed up—but the schedule is every other weekend. An extended schedule in the pro-father state of Texas, it is every other weekend and every fifth weekend as well. This is the standard to be a father? A father is a 50 percent role, fifty-fifty. And so for any father out there who doesn't go and fight that part of it, then what are you doing? Society is part of it, but fathers have the responsibility to take back and fight for what's theirs, and that is to be the father.

Tito Ortiz

UFC HALL OF FAME FIGHTER

AT FIRST I WAS LIKE, "Oh God, what did I get myself into?" My parents were always absent when I was growing up; they were always getting high, and they never showed me the things to become a better person. When I had my first son, Jacob, it was a blessing in disguise because he kind of changed my life. I was the world champion at the time, and I was going down the road of partying all the time; I cheated. I was doing all these things because I never had that attention as a kid, and all of a sudden, being the world champion, I had that attention. I had those things presented to me. I had those opportunities, and I kind of lost myself. Having my son changed all that. My ex and I got divorced, and she moved to Arizona. I've been a part of his life through all of it, and I try to be the best father I possibly can. I try to make sure I don't make the same mistakes that my father did or my mom.

When I was thirteen, I hung around gangs, and that was my family. I could easily have gone down the same path of my father, but just because it happened to you, it doesn't mean it has to continue to happen. Break the cycle, break the chain, and change your life by giving your child what you never had—that's been my mentality of being a father. It's funny how things come full circle, because I had twin boys with my ex, Jenna Jameson, and drugs became a huge issue with her. She used during the pregnancy, and I spent years trying to help her and trying to change her mentality, and I couldn't do it. My mom left my dad because he couldn't get sober, and I left Jenna because she couldn't get sober. I now have 100 percent custody of my twins, and I'm going to do everything possible to be a good father.

Oz Pearlman

MENTALIST, EMMY AWARD WINNER,
AMERICA'S GOT TALENT FINALIST

THE WORDS THAT I WOULD say are the strongest are *joy* and *fulfillment*. Those are the two things I feel with the kids. I get tremendous joy—it doesn't matter what kind of day I had—the moment my son runs up and gives me a hug and gives me a kiss, it doesn't matter. Everything else just melts away. What is fulfilling is seeing them learn, seeing them pick stuff up. It really is kind of like a path to immortality, if you will.

Now, not everyone is gonna be a parent, but it's one of those things that as you see your kid grow up, seeing things through their eyes and getting to experience again what it was like to be a kid and how fun and new everything is, there's just nothing like it—there really truly isn't. Some people are destined to be, and they know from a young age that they're going to be, parents, and they think about it and it's a goal. For me, I didn't really know what I was going to do in terms of having kids, and when we had our first child, it was eye-opening. I realized that this is it: this is what it was meant to be, like everything is for this. It really is the best part of life. I love my wife too—don't get me wrong—but having kids and seeing them grow up together and raising them is just unreal.

Chris Powell

HOST OF *EXTREME WEIGHT LOSS*,

NEW YORK TIMES BESTSELLING AUTHOR

TO BE TOTALLY HONEST, I had been a bachelor for thirty years of my life, and it terrified me because I started to fall deeply in love with this woman, Heidi, who had two children. It scared the heck out of me because I didn't know anything about kids. I didn't know anything about being a father, so for me it was terrifying. But after six, seven, eight months of seeing Heidi with her children and seeing the relationship and connection they had, for me, that was actually one of the most attractive parts about her.

It took a couple of months to sink in, but I realized there's nothing to be scared of at all. That the connection between a parent and a child is such a beautiful thing, and from that point on I realized, hey—this is something that I personally feel like I want to embrace.

As our relationship blossomed, I became a much bigger part of her children's lives, and before you know it, Heidi and I made the decision to become committed to one another, and I accepted the role of father wholeheartedly. I had a huge learning curve to grow on, and, at the time, her kids were two and four, and they taught me the ropes really fast.

David Rutherford

US NAVY SEAL VETERAN

IT WAS SUBSTANTIAL. FOR ME, I was still operational and was working overseas for the agency and missed most of the pregnancy. After my first child was born, thirty days later, I was back out the door for seventy-five days and then on and off for basically the next year and a half. So initially for me, fatherhood and the concept of fatherhood was split mostly with my dedication toward working for the agency, and that took priority. Over the course of the next several years, we had our second daughter, and that's where my frame of mind and what it meant to be a father really began to change. I kept a distance from that reality by being in the life of carrying a gun for a living. But when you are home and you're around it day in and day out, it's much more relative to the demands on your own psyche, and that's where I began to recognize that fifteen years of carrying a gun for a living (Navy SEALs and CIA) was not very conducive to being a good father.

Jim Stroesser

ENTREPRENEUR, CEO OF CALI STRONG

IT CHANGES YOUR PERSPECTIVE COMPLETELY. I couldn't imagine going through life and not having kids. Having children changed my life quite a bit because it wasn't what I thought it would be. I think that's kind of how God works—He gives you challenges that you can handle. I have a son that has Asperger's, and so it was a very difficult childhood but a beautiful childhood all the same. You have to accept what God gives you and make the best out of that. I think we have done that.

My son is extremely bright, which most children with Asperger's are, but he gets caught up sometimes with his obsessive-compulsive behavior, which gets a little difficult for him. He understands it from an intellectual standpoint, but from an emotional standpoint, it's very difficult on him. It's hard on his mother, it's hard on me, and it's hard on him. When you have Asperger's, you are extremely bright but you don't like to socialize, you don't like to talk to people.

But as he got older, he ended up working at one of our stores as a salesclerk, and he became one of our top salespeople. He became so successful that he took a job at Target, and he became their number one salesperson of their credit cards, which is an up sale, a very difficult thing to sell. When he is focused on something, he can do it extremely well. So we have gone through some serious highs and some serious lows, and it's been the biggest challenge of my life.

Ryan Sutter

FIREFIGHTER, FIRST WINNER OF *THE BACHELORETTE*

YOU SORT OF GO BACK and appreciate your own parents for all the stuff they did to create the people we've all become. You appreciate life a little bit differently, when you start to look at it through the eyes of your kids. The entire perspective of adulthood changed when Trista and I had our son and amplified a little bit more when we had our daughter. You go from having more of a self-centered life, not necessarily in a bad way, but the focus of your life when you're single or don't have kids is generally yourself, and then you have these kids who you are responsible for developing into people. That changes everything. It changed everything from the amount of sleep you get to the food you eat to the way that you go on hikes. It was no longer about getting to the top of the mountain—it was sort of simply about just getting as far as you could and enjoying the experience and trying to create these valuable moments with your kids.

Mikey Taylor

PROFESSIONAL SKATEBOARDER, ENTREPRENEUR

I BECAME A DAD A MONTH AFTER my thirtieth birthday. It changed everything. All my friends who do not have kids, I find myself struggling to tell them how impactful and different life is after kids, but if anyone has kids, you know exactly what it is because it flips your world upside down. The things that you valued or thought were important kind of become very secondary, and you have just a new purpose in a sense of who you are and what you are here to do.

By far the biggest struggle that I faced, from a relationship standpoint, was my priorities. For me, my job always came first. I put skating in front of everything, so just the trickle-down effect of being married and trying to have a relationship with my wife and then being a dad, when something else is more important, doesn't really end well. Becoming an entrepreneur presented many similar struggles as skating. I think that goes to my personality; when I do things, I become consumed by them. So, even though being a pro skateboarder is different in a lot of ways than running a business, the obsession and the amount of effort I put toward them are still the same. The thing that I really had to work on was learning how to run a business and have a successful marriage and be a good dad all together. That was the biggest shift, and it is something that wasn't easy for me. I ultimately had to switch my priorities and put my family first and have the business come second.

Benjamin Watson

NFL VETERAN TIGHT END, SUPER BOWL CHAMPION

I'M THE OLDEST OF SIX KIDS and I knew I never wanted to have six, so we just went from five to seven kids, with the twins, and we never landed on six.

I met my wife at the University of Georgia. We dated for several years, and we always talked about having four kids. We got married, waited a few years, and started having kids. We had four kids in literally four and a half years. I knew I wanted to be a dad, but I was scared when we were actually pregnant with our first. It changes your life. People talk about it all the time, how fatherhood changes your life.

I think, for me, there was obviously that sense of responsibility, and not just responsibility of taking care of a baby or a family but of understanding the role of influence that you have on the next generation. It really is powerful. When you are sitting there, holding your newborn child, you're looking in the face of places that you will never go to, because they're gonna outlast you. How are you going to positively affect that child? What are the things you are going to teach him or her? What are you going to pour into them and how are you going to do it? It can be very overwhelming, and I remember feeling overwhelmed, and I still feel that way in a different way now. But it really is a tremendous sense of joy as well because these little children look up to you, and they really need you.

Dana White

UFC PRESIDENT

IT CHANGES EVERYTHING. It changes what you want because it's not about you anymore—it becomes about them. It's the greatest thing you can do, and it makes you realize why we are here. We are here to become parents and raise children. Becoming a father changes you in many different ways and mostly for the positive.

People often ask me about my legacy and what I do for a living. What I do for a living, at the end of the day, means nothing. When your life is over and you're lying there in that box and whoever shows up to your funeral shows up, the only thing that matters, and the only real legacy, is your children. Hopefully, you've lived a life and have done things right, and your kids get up there and say, "He was a great father!" I mean, nothing else matters. Who you were as an employee, who you were as a business owner, or whatever walk of life you chose to pay the bills, the only real legacy you have and the only thing that means anything is what those kids have to say about you.

Matthew Williams

GREEN BERET, MEDAL OF HONOR RECIPIENT

I WAS THIRTY-FIVE OR THIRTY-SIX when I became a dad, and it was a huge change. I was actually on a kind of break; I was instructing one of our advanced skill schools for Special Forces, so I had some time at home, which was good. I've been able to be home for the most part; I've done one deployment since we had our son.

Overall, it changed my whole outlook on the way things are. It reinforced putting family first. My career at that point was always first things first, and I was willing to jump on whatever and do whatever was needed. Of course, I still am, but I always have it in the back of my head, taking into account, raising a young son and making sure that I'm around for as much as I can be, knowing that I still have quite a bit of time left in the military and there will be those times where I definitely won't be able to be around.

Being on deployment is tough, but we have it a bit easier now, to be honest, with all the technological capabilities. To be able to reach back home, doing FaceTime and at least seeing video of the kids, which helps a lot. It's definitely tough, especially with a really young child, which over five or six months, the drastic changes that they're making and knowing that you're not there for it, it's a harder thing to watch. It's always in the back of your mind, you know, what am I missing out on? What's going on? What big milestones are you missing? I've been fortunate and haven't had to miss anything really huge. I missed a Christmas, but he was so young that it wasn't that big of a deal.

Those are the hardest parts though—guys that have older kids, I've seen them miss birthdays and Christmas and those kinds of things constantly, and that's the hardest part, when you miss out on those special moments. But overall, becoming a dad definitely is a huge eye-opener, I'll say that. You think you can prepare for it and all that, but there's no way.

Discipline

"**I**S IT BETTER to be loved or feared?" This question is posed in the movie *A Bronx Tale*, and it comes to mind when I think about disciplining my children. I want my children to love me; that goes without saying. I'd also like to know that my wife could say to them, "Just wait until your father gets home!" and that would summon some sense of fear in them strong enough to behave better in that particular moment.

Love and fear are a balancing act, with the sole intention of leading my children to a state of self-discipline. All four of my kids require slightly different styles of discipline. I have one son that I could spank all day and it wouldn't change anything, while another one I could simply threaten to spank him and that will be enough. I could tell one of my sons not to touch the stove and that will suffice, while another one won't listen until he touches the stove and burns his finger. Finding out the best way to communicate with each child is done by trial and error. My overall goal is for them to take what I'm saying as a direction and not as a suggestion. I also want to eventually build a certain level of trust with them, so they know what I'm making them do is for their own good.

One book I recommend reading to better understand how your children give and receive love is *The 5 Love Languages* by Gary Chapman. I think all couples can benefit from reading this book together, as it's designed to help couples express love for each other in a more genuine way. The five love languages listed in the book are: Words of Affirmation, Acts of Service, Receiving Gifts, Quality Time, and Physical Touch. On the website 5LoveLanguages.com, you can take a quiz with your children as young as five years old. It can be eye-opening and provide helpful insight on how to better handle discipline with your children. For instance, my wife and I discovered that our two oldest boys respond to Words of Affirmation. As a result, we have changed our approach to discipling them by using some words of affirmation, such as, "I love you, but I hate this choice you've made. You're an awesome student, but I don't think you studied as much as you could have for this test. I'm proud of the big brother you are, but because you did that to your sister you are not allowed to play video games tonight." We have also made it a point to use more words of affirmation with them on a day-to-day basis, and the outcome has been more than satisfactory.

Sometimes when I think of the word *discipline*, I have an image of Mr. Strickland from *Back to the Future* calling Marty McFly a slacker. There's no doubt that the way children are disciplined in the school system has changed drastically since 1955. How you discipline children as a parent depends on many factors. A high percentage of the dads I've interviewed on *First Class Fatherhood* have testified that they were spanked as a child. Many go into further detail about being hit with belts or paddles or switches. However, a low percentage admit to spanking their own children, and even the ones who do say it is much different from the way they were spanked.

My father was born in 1930 and didn't have me until he was fifty years old. He came from a completely different world of discipline, and my own style of discipline as a father is much different from his. I have spanked my children, but the feeling I get when I do is so terrible that I don't use it as a primary source of punishment. I often wonder if my dad felt the same way when he spanked me. If he did, he didn't show it. It's one of the questions I would have asked him had he been alive when I became a father.

The way you were disciplined while growing up will certainly affect the way you choose to discipline as a father. Even if your experience was a bad one, you can now correct those mistakes and treat your child the way you wanted to be treated. The way your partner was disciplined will affect their discipline style as well. Making your approaches work cohesively is a challenge worth the effort. A united front presents the best path for your children to have a clear understanding of the rules and what happens if they break them.

Technology has changed immensely since I was a kid, and we use it to our advantage with our kids. For instance, my children would much rather receive an hour of game time for doing their chores than a few dollars. So, at the Lace residence, we use game time as a form of currency. Right or wrong, it works for us, and finding out what works best for you as a dad is the most important thing when it comes to disciplining your children. Below, you'll read the responses from some of the dads I have interviewed, as we discussed discipline.

David Ankin

CEO AND HOST OF *TOYMAKERZ*

I TRY DIFFERENT THINGS. I think every kid is a tad different. My son, I realize, is identical to me. You can't make me do anything, and you're surely not going to make my son do something; he is stubborn. He's my son and I understand that. I talk to him like an adult. I went after my son one time hard to spank him and totally missed him. I totally missed him. I swatted at him hard and, man, you would have thought I beat the kid to death because he knew I was coming.

I talk to him like an adult and I treat him like an adult. I believe in spankings even though I haven't had to do it with my son because that's how I grew up. I only had a few spankings in my life, but that's all I ever needed. I didn't need a bunch. I learned quickly, and my son is the same way. Now he's at the age where I tell him, you know right from wrong, you can make that decision, but understand you might not have that phone tomorrow or have the ability to play video games. Everything is all about a phone or a computer or the internet, and I understand now that that's the society he was raised in, but in the big scheme of things there has to be a happy medium.

He still goes to the shop with me on the weekends and clocks in and out. He wants to work, and he has to do certain jobs at the shop. It's our job as parents, in my opinion, to make sure they get all aspects; you have to be able to work on your car or realize when you bring it to a shop what might be wrong. He has to know how to do laundry and cook food and do the fundamentals of being an adult.

Teddy Atlas

LEGENDARY BOXING TRAINER

WHEN IT CAME TO MY SON, I would play stickball with him, basketball with him, Wiffle ball, and I was the universal every- thing, I was the official pitcher and the official quarterback and everything. Sometimes there would be twenty or thirty kids, and I'd play all day long with them until it got dark, and my son loved it.

I remember when he was five years old, like all kids, he would do something wrong, and my wife would bring it to my attention and say listen, he can't play today. And it would break my heart. I'm in the boxing business, so I'm supposed to know something about being tough. But I wanted to be able to sneak out of that responsibility and let my wife tell him, but you have to be a part- ner with this stuff. So I remember one time I had to tell him and it killed me.

He was in his room and he cried, and then all of a sudden it got quiet. I stayed outside the door and I listened. I heard him talking; he was talking to himself, and I heard him say, "I'm bad! I'm bad!" I opened the door and I was almost in tears. I grabbed him and hugged him, and I said, "You're not bad, bud. You're not bad at all. You're the greatest kid in the world, the greatest son in the world. You made a little mistake and I just want you to be better. I just want to make sure that later, when you get bigger, that you don't make the same mistakes. You're the greatest! Don't ever think you are bad."

It scared the crap out of me. I told my wife about it, and I talked about how we can never take for granted how these kids are feel- ing. Just because we did our part and we think we can walk away and go have dinner and everything is okay, no, you don't know what a kid is feeling. You better find out. You better find out what they're feeling. And obviously without saying it directly, I'm talking about where you hear these terrible things where kids take their lives and you think, oh my God, how could that be possible! It's possible. And that's how it's possible, by not listening, by taking for granted that the kids are okay when they might not be. Listen, ask questions, and talk!

Drew Bledsoe

NFL QUARTERBACK, FOUNDER OF DOUBLEBACK WINERY

WE HAVE VERY CLEAR RULES and very clear consequences if those rules are broken. Those things are all communicated with love and communicated clearly. Because of that, kids understand the rules and know that if they don't break them then life is pretty good.

It's genuinely not very stringent stuff; it's more big-picture things. It's honesty, say what you mean, mean what you say, and do what you say you are going to do. It's as simple as that. At times they have had to learn the consequences of being less than honest with their mother and, oh boy, she is a sweetheart, but if you lie to her, you're in deep trouble. So that was a lesson for our boys that they only had to learn once.

Outside of that, over the years, we have really given them a lot of latitude, and their freedoms just grew with the more trust they earned. The more trust they earned with us, the more freedom they had. With the whole mission being that by the time they are eighteen they are their own person, and they make their own decisions. We're always gonna be there for them to listen and advise and so on, but we really believe that once your child is eighteen it's their life. They get to decide what they're doing, and we just hope that we taught them well enough at that point that they can make good decisions.

Matt Brown

PROFESSIONAL UFC FIGHTER

I WAS A DIFFERENT DISCIPLINARIAN before I had my daughter. She kind of changed that whole scene all around. She's a real firecracker, and with my twin boys, they've always been really great, and they've been easy kids. I haven't had to deal with a lot of discipline because they have been so disciplined naturally.

With my daughter, who recently turned three years old, that's a completely different job. I'm very strict with her now. For the longest time I was sort of just a sap and let her get away with whatever she wanted. My main focus, and I think my boys caught on a little quicker with this, is action and consequence. But I had to crack down on my daughter because she would run through the stores; every single time we went to the store she was like, "Okay, it's time to make Dad chase me." Every time we go to the mall or the airport it's the same thing. She would start scratching other kids or trying to bite other kids, so I really had to crack down. I started implementing the action and consequence thing with her, and now she is starting to catch on.

Having something to keep her occupied, something positive to keep her occupied, makes a big difference, I think. Getting her into the martial arts program at my gym has certainly helped out a lot. The energy just needs to be driven in the proper direction, and she seems to handle it pretty well. I try not to be an overbearing disciplinarian either. I want them to have the freedom to make mistakes.

Rafa Conde

DEA, NARCOTICS, SWAT OFFICER

YOU HAVE TO LISTEN TO what every child is saying, even a six-year-old like my daughter; you have to listen to what they're saying. If you can kind of go in the route where you are communicating with what they are saying and stay on that same wavelength, you will actually start to have a little bit of dialogue. Once that dialogue starts going, you as the adult should be able to lead it somewhere. Lead it somewhere and come back around to what you need to get done.

The last thing I do, especially with my daughter, is go head-to-head with her. Because in reality a lot of times—now don't get me wrong, I am firm and I stand my point—but I do it in a way that is much more conducive. A lot of people like to tell their kids, *ABCD,* and the child is not responding. It's a little bit easier if you guide the conversation and the dialogue to where they need it to go and then come right back around to where you need it to go. It might take thirty seconds of your time, and it will make a huge difference. The same way on the job when we negotiate with guys that want to jump off a bridge or are holding a hostage, you want to be able to hear what they're saying. Listen to what they are saying and redirect the conversation back to where you need it to go.

Terrell Davis

NFL HALL OF FAME RUNNING BACK

MY DAD WROTE THE BOOK on discipline. He was pretty heavy with it. There was a lot that I learned growing up that I loved and that I kind of use a little bit; obviously we can't be as physical with kids anymore. We used to get spankings and whoopings and stuff like that, and you can't do that anymore.

I still take some of the firmness that my dad used. I grew up with five brothers, so there were six boys growing up, so my dad had to have that stern authority, and that's what he did. So I use some of the stuff from my mom, which was a little bit more of the nurturing, and I'll use a little bit from my dad, but I'm very big and strict on listening. Listening and paying attention to what I say. To me that's the difference between life or death. For example, what if we are at a train station and I tell you to stop, and you keep walking and get hit by a train? That may sound severe but that's the way I think. So if you don't listen in small moments then you're not going to listen when it's important.

I use a lot of what I learned in sports to help discipline my kids, but I'm fair and balanced. I'm not just all hammer; I'm love. I want my kids to know that I love them, and I tell them that every single day. No matter what, even when it appears that I am being hard on you, I love you. I think we've struck a pretty good balance with them to have them well rounded. They understand structure, they understand discipline, they understand timing, expectations, and all that stuff as we work with them on all of those different things.

J. P. Dinnell

NAVY SEAL VETERAN

NATURALLY I'M GOING TO DISCIPLINE our fourteen-year-old son differently than my girls who are eight. They have different things in their lives that mean something to them. Our daughters do not have phones; my son has a phone. We made him understand that that phone is not a right, it's a privilege, and we take things away from our kids that we know they enjoy if they don't follow the rules or responsibilities that we give them.

Very rarely do we ever have to spank our kids. They understand and know that we don't play when it comes to this. If they do what we've told them not to do, there is an escalation. Sometimes that escalation leads straight to a spanking, but very rarely do we ever have to do that.

My mom and dad were great parents. They, of course, like every parent out there, they lost their temper, they yelled. But when I step back and think about it, I think, should they have done that, no, but they were never physically or mentally abusive to us, they were never degrading to us. So I look at that and realize that I pushed their buttons and pushed them to a limit that they lost their temper, they lost control of their emotions, and I try to become aware of that myself. I need to be able to check my emotions so I don't lose my temper, because I know that when I lose my temper, I say and do things that I'm not proud of, that I regret. I try to recognize that.

The more calm and collected that you can be in the position as a leader, whether that's the leader of your family or your business, the better you're going to be. Learning to detach is always going to help.

Shane Dorian

PROFESSIONAL SURFBOARDER

I EXPECT A LOT OUT of my kids. I expect them to have great manners and be kind, be honest, and all I really ask for is for them to try hard in school and whatever they want to do; I expect them to really try hard. Besides that, I don't ask for a whole lot.

As far as discipline, for me, I take away a thing they like, which is really hard to do as a parent. They really need boundaries, though, and that's the best thing for them. They don't need a friend, they need parents. That's hard because we all want to be their friends and do fun things with them all the time, but if they mess up or they don't do what they should be doing, it's easy to just kind of cop out and just let them get away with it.

When it comes to things like technology, I try to make it where my kids earn their screen time, and it is very limited, especially on school days. They get very little screen time, and they have to earn it, and I am happy to take it away when they are not doing what they are supposed to be doing. It's funny because I have friends who tell me I'm lucky because I have kids who don't like video games, and I'm like I don't know what you're talking about because my kids like video games a lot, I just don't let them sit on video games all day long. So many parents these days will just give their kid an iPad and just forget about the rest of the day. I really feel like they need boundaries.

Richard Eyre

NEW YORK TIMES BESTSELLING AUTHOR

IT'S OUR ATTITUDES THAT MAKE the difference. When I was a young dad, I used to run a lot. And while I was running, I had four words in my mind that described the kind of dad I wanted to be. And they all start with a *C,* and I would just say them to myself as I was running. The first one is Confidence. I want to give my kids confidence. The second one is Calmness. I want to be calm when I'm around them so they will feel relaxed. The third one is Concentrate. That is concentrate on one at a time, one at a time, because that's how you become a good dad.

The fourth one was to be a Consultant. I was a management consultant in real life and I wanted to be a consultant with my kids in the sense that I don't want to give them all the answers. A good consultant asks a lot of good questions. A good consultant asks, "What do you want to do? What do you think should happen? What do you feel good about?" I wanted to be a dad who guided my kids but didn't push them. To me that means being a consultant and saying it's your goals I want to help you with. I want to be the wind beneath your sails, but I don't want to tell you what to do. I want you to find your own gifts and I want to help you use them.

Micah Fink

NAVY SEAL VETERAN

MY WIFE AND I DEFINITELY discipline in a partnership, but I would say that I am the authoritarian in the family. I always use the example that a leader doesn't demand respect. I don't demand respect from my kids; I command it by who I am and the example I set. I spank my kids, but that is not my first go-to. There's always a level of severity, as firm as necessary.

For instance, if I tell them to do something, it's one time. I'm only going to say it one time. "Go outside, bring the wood in, and stack it by the wood stove!" If my son drifts off and I come in and it's not done, there is no negotiation, he drops down and gets in the push-up position and he stays there. My kids are getting so strong, which means they make a lot of mistakes, they can stay in that position for fifteen minutes, that's how strong they are getting. They stay in that position—no talking—plank position, and then they get up and they go about their business.

Now they know it's just one time; I don't yell, I don't scream, I'm just firm as necessary. If you punch your brother or your brother punches you, then there is the next level of severity. We have a big hill outside my house, and we have a pile of rocks. If we are having an issue and it warrants it, you have to carry one rock and place it on top of the hill, which is a small mountain. When they come back down, they're very tired, and then it's over. We always discuss the lesson and what they learned.

There always has to be recourse, a cause and effect. I grew up with a rough upbringing, and back then it was a beat and release program, which made me operate out of fear. I was afraid of being in trouble, but I feel that the way I teach my kids is this kind of cause and effect, and we always discuss the outcome. But they have to pay the man. You have to train them, but you can't force them. Even when they make a wrong decision, it's a good lesson; but there always has to be a by-product that's only as firm and as fair as necessary. These are lessons that I've learned that I am able to take and reshape and apply to who I am today and help my kids be a better version of themselves.

Branden Hampton

ENTREPRENEUR, *FORBES* #1 RATED INFLUENCER

WE ARE BIG PROPONENTS OF having open discussions in our household. I don't think there's much information that everyone in the house is not privy to. I would say that our children have a great deal of respect for us, but it's a two-way street.

Our house has a structure I relate to the movie *Mean Girls*; it's like we are a cool mom and a cool dad. We are like their friends. We are very modern and very hip. I do social media for a living, so you could imagine how in tune we are with everything pop culture related. We have a group chat with our family that we send memes to. What parents can say that about having a relationship with their kids?

My wife and I are very young. We have a structure where we have rules, and as long as they are followed then there is a mutual respect and we are almost like friends. I think the foundation of a good relationship for a husband and wife is to be friends, and I think a good foundation for parenting is to have rules but still be friends with your children. Most of the time, if there is a disciplinary issue in the household, then people are going to lose privileges. If somebody does something that is way out of whack and very, very wild, then that could result in a belt, and I don't care how old you are.

Mike Haynes

NFL HALL OF FAMER

WHEN I WAS A KID, my parents spanked us. So when my first child was born, I remember when he was about six years old, we were calling him to the dinner table and I said, "Come on, it's time to eat!" And he said, "I don't want to eat!" We repeated this a few times, so I said, "You can't tell me no," and he was like, "No, no, no," and kept going. So I grabbed something, and I spanked him on his hand, and then I felt so bad that I never spanked any of my kids except for the first one.

I realized that I was going to have to find another way. I can't do what my parents did. It is much more difficult to do it the other way. Spanking is easy, but if you have to convince them or you have to talk to them about it, it's a little bit more difficult. I can't say that I'm perfect, I'm sure that I am not perfect when it comes to having these conversations with my kids, but you gotta have them and just be committed to them. I think all of my kids would say that they knew right from wrong. It is not an easy thing to do, to talk about or to deal with, but it is something that you have to do if you want your kids to have good experiences and understand that their behavior matters. Their words matter. All of those things are important.

Pete Hegseth

ARMY VETERAN, FOX NATION HOST,
NEW YORK TIMES BESTSELLING AUTHOR

ONE OF THE BIGGEST COMPLIMENTS I got a couple of months ago was that the rumor in the neighborhood is that Pete is a tough disciplinarian. You don't get away with anything at his house. Which I love, so it's not just my kids but it's my friends' kids, whom I love and respect. And we have fun when they are here. But yeah, I am a disciplinarian, probably even more so than my dad, whom I revere.

If there was one thing I came out of my high school years with: I was a little soft and not quite ready for the sharp edges of the modern world. I want to take care of my kids and ensure they are okay at one level; we also need to start fortifying them to be gritty, to be tough, to take risks, to stand up to bullies, and not just call for a mediator and cower in the corner. I have rules and I enforce them mercilessly for what time you have to be home, you gotta clean the basement every night, the chores that you have to knock out, you have to make your bed every morning, you have to say please and thank you, you ask to be excused from the table, and there are consequences if you don't.

I think when you give good parameters to kids, they respond really well. They just need left and right limits, and when they have that then they have a road map to excel. And that's a challenge in a blended family when you have stepkids and kids and finding a balance of how you manage those relationships; I'm not gonna tell you I have that all figured out. You manage your own emotions and start to learn who the kids are and how they respond, but the more fair you are about the rules for everybody, it sort of creates a coherence to the whole group, which is what we're going for.

Dean McDermott

ACTOR—*OPEN RANGE*

I AM THE BAD COP. My wife, Tori Spelling, is the good cop, which is great because it balances us out. I believe in structure and consequences, so I usually enforce that pretty hard. Sometimes maybe too hard, so that's why it's good that Tori is the good cop, and it balances things out and we are a pretty good team. That's what you have to be with your partner—you have to be on the same page as far as discipline and that stuff goes.

The technology is a battle that is waged daily. We are in competition with these screens and our children. We only give them a certain amount of time on them; of course, we have all of the parental blocks on all the computers and phones so they can only see age-appropriate stuff. But it's more about the amount of time that they spend on it, and it seems like every day it becomes more and more as they become, I hate to say it, addicted to these handheld computer screens that they can play games on and search stuff on.

I try to get them to use it for education purposes. If they want to play games I would rather them go on ABCmouse to start using it to get education instead of entertainment. We put restrictions on the amount of time they use them, and we try to guide them into productive viewing. I have never personally liked video games and have always felt like they were a colossal waste of time, but it's a struggle for any parent. If you have a partner that's on the same page as you, it works really well.

Brad Meltzer

NEW YORK TIMES BESTSELLING AUTHOR

I DON'T KNOW IF THIS is right or if this is wrong; I don't think there is a right or wrong answer most of the time. I think being a good father means you have to figure things out. I want my kids off their screens, I want them off of their devices, and the only way to do that is you have to give them something better. That's why we launched the *I Am* series of books.

But when I can't beat them, I join them. Last night I was playing *Fortnite* with my kids. I am terrible at it and I get killed in a second and they all laugh at me, but when I was a kid growing up, I loved comic books and I loved to read. My dad was a big sports guy. I like sports, too, but my dad liked sports more than I did; I liked science fiction more.

But you know what my dad did? Now he much rather would have been buying baseballs for me, but he was always buying me comic books. He bought me what I loved. He met me halfway and said, "Okay, you love this stuff. I think it's kind of crap, but if you love it, then I'm in." That was a beautiful lesson my dad gave me, so I just try and use that lesson today as well with my own kids.

I think there is only one rule to be a dad—you just gotta love your kids. You're going to screw up a million times, we all screw up a million times, but the only thing you can't screw up is you have to make sure your kids know you love them. That's it. Everything else you're gonna mess up. Love your kids with all your might, and the rest will take care of itself.

Michael Muller

AWARD-WINNING PROFESSIONAL PHOTOGRAPHER

I CAME UP WITH THE spanking and the paddles and the belts. I came up in that world, but I do not take that approach as a disciplinarian. I discipline my kids with, especially nowadays, the phone, because there is not a lot of leverage I have with my kids. But if I take away the electronics, I can get some leverage. So that is a great tool, and it's almost like we gave them phones so we could take them away.

What I do know is the more you try to control your kids, or the more I tried to control my kids, the more they are going to rebel. The more they are going to try and push their will. So I felt like if I was like that with my daughter, she would be climbing outside the window with the quarterback doing what I don't want her to be doing. So I do not shame or yell at my kids when they have done something that I am not pleased with. When I tell them I am disappointed, it crushes them more than any spanking I could do.

I spend a lot of time with my kids. I've pretty much been to every game, and many times I am the only dad there. I talk with them, and what that has done with my sixteen-year-old! If any of you have tweens, you'll know what I'm talking about—once they hit that thirteen, fourteen age mark, they become completely different people. Social life comes into play and all of that, and what I don't get is the hand. I don't get the door shut on me.

I talk with my kids about vaping and the kids who are vaping, drinking, and the things that are really going on that a lot of kids don't talk to their parents about. I don't want to be my daughter's friend or an extreme disciplinarian; I want to be balanced in the middle. I want to have a trusting relationship where the communication is key so I know what's going on in her life because not knowing is the worst. If you don't put that time in at the beginning, it is so much more difficult when they get older to try and earn that relationship.

Ross Patterson

ACTOR, PRODUCER, HOST OF *DRINKIN' BROS* PODCAST

I'LL SPANK AND TIME-OUT. If you scream or cry in a restaurant, you're getting taken home. If my kid talks back to me, he's going in time-out. If he pushes his brother down or knocks him down the stairs, he's gonna get a spanking for that.

Some parents aren't cool with that, but that's how I was raised and that's what I believe in, so that's what I do. That's what works for me and my wife. Is that right for everybody? Not necessarily. It's a different world as far as parenting goes, and I've seen it both ways. I haven't seen any positive results from just sitting there and letting your kids do what they want. I don't subscribe to that, "Oh, it's a different time than when we grew up." It's not. Family values are still family values, and the way you're raised will determine, more than likely, the person you're going to be in life.

Just because we have different electronics now, iPads and things like that, doesn't mean you change as people, and it doesn't change discipline style within you. And I'm raising my kids the same way I was raised. I came from loving parents. I don't have a bad word to say about my childhood, but yeah, I was spanked and I was in time-out if I did things wrong. Same with my kids; they're gonna know about it. I'm not going to treat them any different because society is starting to. I just hate this soft mentality that is out there in the world today. If you raise them like that, first of all, they're gonna run all over you; second of all, they'll probably be living in your house until they're thirty-three years old, which is not healthy either.

Richard Phillips

MERCHANT MARINER CAPTURED BY SOMALI PIRATES

MY FATHER WAS LIKE VINCE LOMBARDI on a bad day. He was a football coach and teacher with eight kids, and he was always working. He was very tough, but you knew exactly where you stood with my father.

One thing I wanted to do was hug my kids, and that's one thing my father never really did with me. I wanted to be open and show my kids that we can be open, because I think that allows them to be open to you. I was tough. I was always reciting little sayings and witticisms, and I would say them multiple times because I think it takes multiple times to get through to a younger-than-seven-year-old's brain. My kids would finish the sentences, they were so sick of hearing it.

I was tough from the outset, but I knew that the most important thing for kids, I think, is to allow them to be kids. I wasn't a yeller. I've been criticized about that sailing as a captain by people who worked under me who told me I need to yell more. But I'm not a yeller. When I get mad, I get quiet. I hate a yeller; my father was a yeller and a curser and a swearer. Working on the ocean after twenty years, I got tired of swears, because every other word is an F-bomb. So basically, with our kids, we tried to show an example, tell them an example, and then let them see through their own way how to act.

Neil Riordan

PHD, APPLIED STEM CELL RESEARCH

MY FATHER WAS AGAINST any sort of corporal punishment, so he would never spank us. He was a psychiatrist, so he was very antispanking, but yet we went to school in my day, and we got the hell beat out of us by our teachers, gym teachers, etcetera. Now that's all banned, but when I was in school that was still a part of the deal, and nobody ever said a word. Now you couldn't even look at a kid funny without getting written up or something. It's a different world.

So I never was a spanker with my kids; it was more of a time-out deal. I like the carrot better than the stick, too, so we set up goals for them for certain milestones, and they would get rewarded. That always worked better for me. I've been lucky because that has made them self-starters. I have a really good friend of mine whose son in school just does not thrive, and he spends an inordinate amount of time trying to motivate him, and I never had that challenge.

David Rutherford

NAVY SEAL VETERAN, FOUNDER OF TEAM FROGLOGIC

OUR DISCIPLINE IS THAT WE really drill down on manners, we drill down on being respectful, we drill down on being accountable for your things and yourself. I inspect beds every morning, or try to. We expect good table manners and really just drill down on the basics. Those things are substantial. We have seventeen rules that we created that the girls pretty much recite every time we're driving them to school. These rules enable the girls to start developing their framework.

I will say that I am a former Navy SEAL, so sometimes I'll lose my temper enough to where I'll raise my voice unnecessarily in a circumstance because I get frustrated. We do fun disciplinary things like push-ups and air squats, but with harsh discipline we will isolate, let them calm down, and then go in for the teaching moment afterwards.

The main idea of my motivational entertainment company, Team Froglogic, is confidence. I focus on four main ideas whether I am working with kids or working with corporations or anyone; and the four fundamental pillars of Froglogic are: learning how to embrace fear, forging your self-confidence every day, living a team life, and living with purpose, ultimately trying to find out why am I here and what is my meaning.

Marshall Sylver

HYPNOTIST, MAGICIAN

NOT EXPECTING SOMEBODY to measure up, especially our children, is an insult. So the basis of this is consistency and predictability. My kids are amazing. I don't say that just because they are my kids; they are amazing, and when we go out in public, we get compliments all the time. Other parents will come by and say, "What did you do to get your kids to be so well behaved?" The fact of the matter is, we are consistent. We consistently make them be respectful, we consistently expect them to say thank you. We consistently expect them to introduce themselves with confidence and with a great amount of respect for people.

Because of that, because we have an expectation of them to measure up, because we use specific language patterns . . . A lot of time parents will tell their kids what not to do, and we don't do that, we tell them what to do. My wife and I have very different parenting styles. She negotiates with them a bit and I don't. I'm direct. That has a bit to do with me being a hypnotist for a number of years, but I also think that once kids know how to win, then they win.

I have a little technique that I use whenever they're behavior is less than desirable. I'll look at them and I'll ask, "What am I about to say?" and they'll say, "Stop running in the house." I say, "What am I about to say?" They answer, "Get your elbows off the table." So what that does is it reinforces them knowing what the desired behavior is, and also it gets them to come to their own conclusion of what they should be doing in that moment. After a while, you don't have to tell them anymore.

Eric Trump

EXECUTIVE VICE PRESIDENT
OF THE TRUMP ORGANIZATION

THE HARDEST ASPECT OF FATHERHOOD that I am going to struggle with—and I'm new in this game, having only been a father for a couple of years—is to find that balance between being a father and a mentor, versus being a friend. Those two roles have to work in conjunction but don't always align. You don't always want to play the role of friend because as a father, you need your child's respect and the ability to discipline, but at the same time you want your child to love you, enjoy you, and want to be around you. It is a balance I hope to achieve.

Despite the stereotypes often imparted on wealthy families, I am a person who firmly believes in making my children work. It is one of the best traits my father instilled in me, Don, and Ivanka. When we were eleven years old, we began working on construction sites every free moment we had for minimum wage. We were cutting re-bar with acetylene torches, we were doing electrical work, tile work, digging ditches, demoing walls, cutting down trees, mowing lawns, and virtually every other hands on construction job one could do. There is no question that those years laid the foundation for what we do, and who we are today. My father made us work. He did not believe in idle hands. Nothing good comes from boredom. Unfortunately, you see a lot of other kids who just don't work, don't have jobs, and have far too much free time. I have plenty of friends who did not have jobs, did not have structure. Their free time, more often than not, led to bad habits—drinking, drugs, and worse. My father was a big believer in "you're gonna work for minimum wage, you will understand the value of a dollar, and you're gonna learn a trade."

My father's motto was simple—teach your children a true work ethic, teach them a skill, occupy their time, and make them so tired after work that they pass out early. Do not allow them the time to be corrupted. Make the cost of that beer . . . or worse . . . so significant and painful that money is saved and allocated to something so much more important and meaningful.

Jeff Utsch

NAVY SEALS SWIM INSTRUCTOR

EACH CHILD, I HAVE LEARNED, does not require the same parenting skills. It is not a machine where you do this or you check off this; they come here all different. Some are more obedient and want to please. Some are less obedient and really don't care what you think. They can be from the same mom and dad, the same environment, yet they all come a little bit different. So it is more of an art than a science.

It is worth taking time to sit down and talk with your spouse and talk with your children and think about what would be best for them. Accountability is important, to have them be raised in an environment of accountability and of tough love, of facing consequences, of learning right and wrong, of not having mom and dad always save you from yourself but being able to do that in an environment where you have a safety net for a while. Because eventually there is no safety net, and they will be fully responsible to society for their actions.

The two rules that we had with our kids growing up, other than household chore rules and general behavior rules, was they had to play a sport and an instrument. It was up to them which instrument or sport to play, but they had to choose that. Our oldest played soccer and the piano, our second did karate and plays the violin, our third played soccer and plays the guitar, and our youngest is into gymnastics and plays the piano. I think all of those skills and talents can last with you through your whole life and give you confidence.

Jason Weaver

ACTOR, SINGER—*THE LION KING*

THERE ARE TIMES WHEN I have to lay down the law and let my son know that "Hey, I'm your father, you're my son. I'm a grown man and you're a young man." There are times where you just have to give that look to remind them. I just talk to my son and lay out the pros and the cons, and I will use my own example by saying, "Hey, when I was faced with the same situation, this is what I did, and I really messed that up. Don't make the same mistake that I made. I'm not telling you this because I haven't done it. I'm telling you because I've done it and it doesn't work so don't do it."

So usually when I talk to my son like that, he knows that I'm coming from a real and genuine place where I am trying to save him the trouble of going through things, but at the same time, kids are going to be kids, especially teenagers. There are times where he still has to bump his head and learn on his own. What I just try to do is make sure that those situations where he does bump his head, it doesn't cause any irreparable damage or hurt him seriously. I'm a believer in God and I pray a lot, asking God for guidance as a father so I can instill the right things in my son to ultimately make him a better man than me.

Jocko Willink

NAVY SEAL VETERAN AND
NEW YORK TIMES BESTSELLING AUTHOR

MY PARENTS BOTH WORKED WHEN I was growing up, so there was a lot of leeway of what I could get away with doing and the way that I behaved. I didn't really abuse it. I was a rebellious kid, but I wasn't anything that was too crazy. So I would say that my parents gave me a lot of leeway, and I do the same thing with my kids.

As my kids get a little bit older, they can do whatever they want as long as it is good for their long-term benefit. If they are doing something that is starting to get out of line, then I will talk to them about it. If you were to ask me what type of discipline I use with my kids, I would say my primary tool with my kids is that I ask them questions. I'll sit down and ask them questions, such as, "Why are you doing that? What are you expecting to happen? What outcome are you looking for there? How is this gonna benefit you in the long run?" So for me that's normally enough for my kids to realize that maybe they're not making a good decision and they'll straighten back out.

Fitness and Health for Dads and Kids

TRANSFORMATION TAKES PLACE when you become a father. As with most transformations, it doesn't happen overnight. This transformation happens within your mind, body, and spirit. It begins the moment you find out your spouse or partner is pregnant.

We often hear about moms who suffer from postpartum depression and deal with body image issues after childbirth. New dads face similar challenges, as we focus all our attention on the needs of our newborn and our partner. In most cases, if the mom is a working mom, she'll have paid time off for maternity leave, and rightfully so. But that's often not the case for dads. After having this life-changing experience, in which we're constantly questioning whether we're ready, whether we can afford kids, and being hyper vigilant to the needs of our young families, we're expected to get back to work.

Most jobs, such as mine on the railroad, will compensate you for three days of bereavement for the loss of an immediate family member but offer no leave for the birth of a new child. I was given three days' pay to bury and grieve my mom and three days' pay to bury and grieve my father but no days to welcome and celebrate my first or any of my children. Three days for death and none for new life.

Going back to work after each of these experiences was unique. Everyone around me was continuing with their normal lives and regular routines, yet my entire world was completely altered. If you're the first person among your friends to have kids, you may begin to feel a bit isolated from them. A transformation is happening, and your friends will notice.

I strongly suggest that you don't resist the change. Allow it. Allow yourself to move with the tide of paternity. The great poet Rumi once said, "Try not to resist the changes that come your way. Instead, let life live through you. And do not worry that your life is turning upside down. How do you know that the side you are used to is better than the one to come?"

I'm on the other side, and it is far better than I could've ever imagined. But that didn't happen overnight. Spending time with your friends, going to the gym, going to sporting events, and other activities will become less frequent. Over the course of the first year of becoming a father, many things will change, including the amount of sleep you get. Sleep deprivation can cause several health problems.

As you focus on your new family and transition into the role of father, you cannot neglect your health. The term "dad bod" has become a popular one, a mix between a muscular and an overweight physique. Sleep, diet, and exercise may easily fall to the wayside in the first few years of fatherhood.

I've had the honor of speaking with many health and fitness professionals on *First Class Fatherhood*, and they've given some incredible advice for new dads about how to stay fit, eat healthy, and teach your children to do the same. Along with our own health, our children's health and wellness is a top priority. In this age of technology, keeping kids fit and active can be challenging. Getting them involved in sports has its benefits, but one major concern for many fathers, me included, is whether to allow our kids to play tackle football, especially with the movie *Concussion* and all the reports about chronic traumatic encephalopathy (CTE). I address this important topic in this chapter, since I've had the opportunity to speak with several former NFL players.

So here are the responses from some of the dads as we discussed physical and mental health, for both dads and their children, diet and nutrition, and the decision as to whether playing contact sports is right for your child.

Joe Arko

STRENGTH AND CONDITIONING COACH

IF YOU ARE A DAD who is looking to lose weight and decide to use a personal trainer, then there are certain things I recommend you consider. I think, number one, you need to look at personality. When you are looking to hire a personal trainer, you are basically agreeing to go on like fifty to a hundred dates over the next six to twelve months. So get to know that person. Go through a good consultation. Look at their track record, testimonials, ask to speak with some of their clients.

Make sure that that trainer is right for your goals or your limitations. Maybe that trainer is fantastic at CrossFit, but you don't want that. Maybe they're fantastic at power lifting or muscle building, but that's not what you want. They may be highly qualified, but make sure it is someone you get along with and enjoy seeing and spending time with, and also make sure they specialize in the specific problem that you are looking to solve.

Not all personal trainers are built equally; they are not all as skilled, and they all have different personalities. Do some homework, look for some credentials, and speak to some of the people they worked with in the past to see what they liked about their experience and if that is similar to what you are looking for as well, before jumping into a commitment with someone for a long period of time.

Mark Bell

PROFESSIONAL POWER LIFTER, INVENTOR

I REALLY LIKE TO COOK for my children. I cook breakfast for them almost every single morning. To me, cooking for your children is important because I'm a nutrition freak and a health freak in a certain sense. When you're talking about having a child and bringing a child into this world, we are talking about nourishment. This is a literal way of providing nourishment for your children . . . I made you this nutritious food so you can have the best possible day you can. I'm not going to be lazy about it, because if I love you, I'm not going to give you a sticky bun and chocolate milk in the morning and send you off to school and think that you'll do well, be healthy, and be happy. I'm not being judgmental toward others that may do that; there's always going to be times where you are going to be a bit more relaxed about some of these things. Of course, you are going to allow your kids to enjoy ice cream, pizza, and do things that other children do. But at the same time I think you should teach them all the principles that you believe in that have helped you in your life.

My son likes to have soda with dinner. He is allowed to have the soda, but I tell him you either pick the soda or you pick the dessert. It's up to him to choose, but I don't allow him to have both because these things can add up very quickly in our lives. So I want to see my kids be healthy, strong, and happy.

Jerome Brown

PERSONAL CHEF TO THE STARS

NUTRITION IS REALLY THE DICTATOR of how your life is going to turn out. Oftentimes, we do things as a direct result of nutrition and our diet. I have been a personal chef for a number of professional athletes, NBA stars, entertainers, movie stars—you name it—and for years I was the go-to chef for those people to keep their weight intact and get them ready for any upcoming movie roles or album photo shoots or what have you. I was the go-to chef and would give them quality five-star meals made to their specifications and keep them within the balance of what they were trying to achieve with a healthy lifestyle, because nutrition is everything.

America has become such a fast-paced, microwave society where everybody wants everything right now. But if we think back to the time where we as a family would come around the dinner table and talk about the events of the day, talk about ideas, talk about moments that needed direction or correction. That's where your conversations are happening. I think that if we come back around the table and have those moments as a family, from a proper eating standpoint, I think a lot of the problems that we have in the world right now we could do away with. I think a lot of the problems that we have can be solved at the dinner table.

Adam Busby

REALITY TV STAR OF *OUTDAUGHTERED*

THAT FIRST COUPLE OF YEARS after having quintuplets it was just a huge shock to the system. It was tough, and little by little I felt like the way that I was, the way I interacted with people, the way I interacted with friends just started to change. I started to get an idea that something was wrong with me because I wasn't acting like myself. I started to just withdraw from a lot of things that made me happy at the time. Even just going to the gym—I didn't have the drive and the ambition to do stuff like that anymore.

My wife, Danielle, started to see a change, and we were talking about stuff throughout this whole process, but it's one of those things where I've never struggled with any kind of depression or anything like that, so I didn't really know a whole lot about it. I feel like people's natural reaction to something that they don't know about is, they're scared of it and they try to hide it and suppress it and push it away and hide it from other people, and so I started to do that. I tried to suppress it and not talk about it; and it only made it worse. It steadily got worse and worse and worse over the course of a year and a half to two years.

Things finally got to a point where my wife sat me aside and pretty much said you gotta get help. You have to go talk to somebody and figure out what is going on. That started me on a journey of going to speak with a church pastor, who recommended I go and speak with a counselor. As I started talking about it and getting it off my chest, that is when I started to see progress. I started to come out of it a little bit and start accepting it. That's when I felt like I got better and turned a corner.

Joe De Sena

FOUNDER OF SPARTAN RACE

I DON'T THINK IT IS the kids that have to change their mindsets. I think it is the parenting. Food, all kinds of food, mostly junk food, is at our fingertips every day. Kids have video games and phones accessible to them all day, every day. So, unless you are parenting and going against the grain of society—right, because you are going to have an upset kid when you're pushing him outside and you're getting him to work out every day and you're giving him only healthy foods when all their friends have a different lifestyle, different parenting styles.

You have to be that parent, the parents we are trying to be. Our kids were out at six this morning in a very cold Boston area pushing sleds and dragging chains. I'm sure the neighbors and their friends thought they were nuts, but that's what we do. Our family pushes hard and tries to eat healthy. You gotta be a hard parent because kids will push back. It's really about how committed you are as a parent with this philosophy. The kid always wins if you don't take a stand.

I was a parent who ran with our kids in the stroller and got them to run at a young age. In fact, when our oldest was eight, he ran the Boston Marathon. When his brother was seven, he ran the New York Marathon. It wasn't just pushing them in a stroller; it was getting them out there to run as well. Although that sounds strange and I sound like some crazy parent, the reality is that in some parts of the world kids will walk eight or ten miles to school. So it's no big deal. The only reason it seems like a big deal is because we sit on a couch all day.

Stan Efferding

PROFESSIONAL BODYBUILDER AND POWER LIFTER

I DON'T HAVE ANY OF the crappy foods in my house such as cookies, cake, candies, juices, and the like. We have plenty of fruits and vegetables and whole foods for our kids to eat. So I try to get them to eat what I eat and take them on ten-minute walks with me. I have a gym in my garage and have them come out when I'm exercising to play so they can see from my example that that's a healthy lifestyle.

Healthy lifestyle habits such as improving your sleep and getting adequate whole food nutrition, using good quality vial available micronutrient dense foods—I think we've come far enough now that I can actually say that red meats, eggs, and whole milk actually build young bodies and young athletes. The science now is much more supportive of the fact that kids need these things to grow and develop. Girls in particular need the iron, the B-12, and the zinc that's in red meats. Young boys and girls need the cholesterol that's important for all the hormone production in the body.

I work hard to make sure I give out good advice regarding lifestyle habits and how important that is for progress for young athletes and young kids. I don't think supplements have an additional benefit. I think they are inferior to whole foods by a long shot. When you use those in place of whole foods, I don't think you get as good of results. As far as performance-enhancing drugs, I don't think there is any place for it for teenagers. They already have adequate hormone levels far and above what adults have. Plus it will shut down their systems if young boys use testosterone in high school, and they will never fully recover. So I avoid all of that stuff with kids. I don't think they need it.

I am also cautious with overtraining, especially with young girls. Overtraining young girls can result in amenorrhea, which is an absence of the menstrual period. There are adverse effects from overtraining in young boys, too, who in wrestling try to cut their weight, which can stunt their growth in the short term acutely. It's not a good idea for them to be overly restrictive. I'm real cautious with making sure they get a complete, well-rounded diet. Those are my recommendations for kids.

Heath Evans

NFL VETERAN RUNNING BACK

WHEN CONSIDERING TO LET YOUR child play tackle football, I would challenge parents to go and research for themselves what the truth is. And it's a sad day we live in where sometimes it is hard to find the truth.

I played flag football at five, six, and seven, and then at eight years old I put the pads on. So if you take a kid at seven or eight years old, he is going to hit another kid in practice at maybe one mile an hour, maybe two miles an hour. At age twelve he's going to be hitting at four or five miles an hour. At fourteen or fifteen in varsity football, some of those collisions could be at sixteen or seventeen miles an hour.

The basic evolution of an athlete is his body being tempered to get hit at one mile an hour or two miles an hour and then three or four and five or six miles an hour, and gradually there's a growth process of the body learning to be able to handle the wear and tear of varsity football. Not only the head but the bone structure, the back and the neck. So if you hold your son out until he is fourteen and then put him on the field with a guy like me who has been playing tackle football since I was seven, he is at a disadvantage from the jump.

And I will say this: nutrition, nutrition, nutrition. Our food is hot garbage. Kids are drinking Gatorade and sodas and all this other crap. There is a major effect of our food being stripped of all its nutrients, so if parents can afford to feed their kids organic and get them good fruits and vegetables and make them eat chicken, other meats, and fish, the brain and our body are amazing. Our body can heal itself of almost anything, as long as you're not taking the game of football and compounding it with drugs and alcohol and beating it up on both ends. In the end I took care of my body, and my body took care of me.

David Harris Jr.

CEO, UNCORKED HEALTH AND WELLNESS

WITH THE CORONAVIRUS PANDEMIC, health and wellness are on the minds of every parent, and for kids one of the biggest things we've been hearing is to teach them to wash their hands constantly and keep their hands away from their face. As far as building up their immune system, good vitamin C is gonna have good absorption in their body. Vitamin C is one of those great old ingredients that we can consume on a regular basis and you really can't get too much of it to build up the immune system. Echinacea is another powerful one to do that, as well as garlic.

The stronger the immune system is, then if someone does contract the coronavirus, the more likely it's just gonna pass.

Anytime you are taking any kind of vitamin, if it is hard to break down or if you can't break it in half, the problem is their coating is so strong that before a lot of those vitamins break down and start to absorb into your body's system, they are about to go out of your body. A lot of us end up taking things that we don't get any benefits from.

So you want to make sure it has good absorption factors. I have a mineral multivitamin supplement called Revive that you can easily break in half. Revive helps to build your body at a cellular level from the inside out, and it gives your body almost everything else it needs mineral- and vitamin-wise.

A lot of vitamins, you can't even break them in half. Gel caps and capsules are always better than tablets. If it is a tablet, you want to make sure you can break it in half, or it shows that it has a very fast release coating on the outside. There definitely is a lot of garbage out there. All ingredients are not created equal. There are thousands of suppliers for each and every individual ingredient, and unfortunately there is nothing that regulates the testing for how potent or how strong those ingredients are, if they were grown with the right nutrients, if they had enough water, or if they had enough light. All of those things factor in to whether or not those ingredients are going to have a good impact on your body and give your body what they should.

When you take ingredients from supplements that have high potency and purity, then your body will normally feel it, notice it, and give you a result that you can acknowledge and benefit from.

Ryan Harris

NFL VETERAN CENTER, SUPER BOWL CHAMPION

WHEN IT COMES TO PARENTS deciding whether or not to allow their kids to play contact football, I am a firm believer that no one should be playing tackle football until the age of fourteen. Let me give you a couple of reasons why.

When I got to the University of Notre Dame, I saw something I had never seen before. I'm talking about a six-foot-six offensive tackle who is 320 pounds. I mean this kid is going in the first four rounds of the NFL Draft if he just tries. And he didn't. I asked him what he was doing, and he told me he was tired of football. Since he got his scholarship, he shut it down. Before he even got to Notre Dame he was done because he had been playing football since he was five.

I would say 80 percent of the players I played with were burned out by the time they finished their second year of college. That's not just with football, that's with basketball, baseball, volleyball, swimming. So the big thing with me is you have to let your kids have fun. You want to play football, great, join a flag football league. You have to create opportunities for them to just have fun with sports.

If your kids want to play football, I would say take them to games. That was the biggest thing for me when I was younger. I learned to love the game first. If you want your kid to play tackle football, wait until puberty because when you do play football, let me tell you what, guys like me are coming to rip your bleeping head off. And we don't care about your feelings, and we don't care what happens to you afterwards. Don't put your kid in that situation, a situation you weren't willing to be in most of the time, and force them to do something they don't want to do, because you could kill their love for the game.

Chris Henderson

GUITARIST FOR 3 DOORS DOWN

I'VE BEEN CLEAN AND IN RECOVERY for over ten years. When I was using and addicted, I was real thin as most addicts are. Once I got clean, I ballooned and bulked up. I gained a bunch of weight and was up to almost three hundred pounds. Basically, I removed drugs and alcohol and replaced it with food. There was no learning curve; it was a 100 percent replacement. I went from cocaine to pizza overnight, and I never looked back.

When I talked to my sponsor, he told me to give it time and let it play out. He said to get some clean time before I address the food thing. So I was still unhealthy. I stayed in recovery for eighteen months before I started addressing the food problem. I made a decision that I needed to learn how to be healthy because I didn't know how to be healthy. I didn't have any healthy kind of life skills at all. All I knew was just go, go, go.

I started researching on the internet, watching documentaries, and I stopped drinking milk and went vegan for about three years. I lost a hundred pounds as a vegan, but I still wasn't satisfied with health. I started distance running and kind of got addicted to distance running.

I still didn't feel healthy or look healthy, and one day a friend of mine came over and he was wearing a CrossFit shirt. I asked him what CrossFit was, and he told me it was hard to explain so why don't you just come with me. I immediately joined a CrossFit gym along with my wife, and I have done it five days a week since then.

I think the personality type that people have who get addicted to things can be used for good if you try. I'm so addicted to CrossFit and being healthy that now I sleep eight hours a day, I'm a better father, I'm a better person, I'm a better bandmate, I'm a better husband. And these habits that I replaced my addictions with are rubbing off on my children now.

Jason Khalipa

CROSSFIT WORLD CHAMPION

IF I WERE RESTRICTED TO doing just one exercise a day, I would choose dumbbell thruster, or a burpee if you have no equipment. You drop to the floor, do a push-up, and stand back up again. If I had equipment or access to dumbbells, I would do dumbbell thrusters where I squat down, stand, and press it over my head. And really what I'm thinking about is movements that move my body with a long range of motion.

I fell in love with CrossFit and the idea of racing against the clock and seeing how many reps you can do in that particular time. I recognized that you can get more work done in less time, and that really fired me up. I try to lay a foundation with my kids in a very soft way about exercise, which I think is important. I think one way we can show our children hard work is through showing them by working out in your garage or at the gym. Kids don't know what it means to work hard in the sense of answering emails or being on phone calls, but they do know what it means to work hard when they are watching you bust your butt and sweat in your garage. Hopefully that will translate, later on, into them knowing that if you want to get in better shape, you gotta put in the work.

Ronnie Lott

NFL HALL OF FAME DEFENSIVE BACK

THE QUESTION FACING MANY PARENTS is when to allow their kids to play tackle football. To me, with today's game, if you are worried and you think that you should not allow it to happen, then take precautions.

My son Isaiah asked me what I think about him playing with pads on, and I asked him what he thought. He told me he liked playing touch, and so he played with his friends and enjoyed it that way. My other son, Ryan, when he was coming out of high school, I didn't think he would be the kind of man he is today with the size that he has. So you never know. He did go on to playing linebacker in the National Football League. You may feel like there will be a time when your child is strong enough or sturdy enough to be able to play.

I would never trade the experience of being with young men. The reason why Boy Scouts was so amazing is that you are around young men. You get a chance to understand the challenges and the difficulties. I think the game of football is about the relationships and the friendships; it's not about what we see in terms of competition. I've always felt there is nothing better than being around great men and learning from them and understanding the issues, the challenges, and the problems. I think that kids should learn about the game of football. I think they should learn about the game of life and having great relationships, knowing that you have people you can count on, who support you, and whether you win or lose, you win together or you lose together, and you find ways to deal with those losses and you find ways to deal with those wins.

Drew Manning

CREATOR OF *FIT2FAT2FIT*

PEOPLE'S PERCEPTION OF HEALTH and fitness is that it needs to be this end-all, be-all thing where they sacrifice themselves, their body, in the gym. It means they are suffering, and they think it sucks and their body is supposed to be sore, and they starve themselves so they are suffering, wanting to look a certain way, thinking if I look this way then I'll be able to love myself, people will love me, people will respect me more. We wait until we have this perfect body until we give permission to love ourselves or accept ourselves.

What happens is it is a lot harder than people think. It's more of a mental and emotional journey, and they get burned out on killing themselves in the gym and starving themselves to look skinny, and then they realize this is so much effort for minimal results. That's their perception of health and fitness: they think they need to be this Instagram model to be of value or be successful at being healthy.

But at the end of the day, especially if you are a parent, it is so important for you to realize that you can't pour from an empty cup. If you are not taking care of yourself first and foremost, it's hard to continue to give and give and give so much to your kids that you sacrifice your own well-being; so at the end of the day, they are pouring from an empty cup. You are a better version of yourself when you take care of your health first. It will catch up to you if you don't realize that lesson. You don't need to go to the gym for hours and ignore your kids while you're meal prepping, but find ways to include your kids in this healthy lifestyle so that they pick up on those habits.

Joel Marion

ENTREPRENEUR, BESTSELLING AUTHOR, PODCASTER

WHEN TRYING TO GET OUR KIDS interested in health and fitness, it is really about making health and fitness a part of their daily routine. Obviously, we live in a very electronically driven age. I remember when I was a kid, we played outside all the time, and we got health and fitness by playing and that was the norm. We would go to the playground and ride our bikes to our friend's house. Nowadays, kids are more consumed electronically with TV and iPads and Netflix and all these types of things.

We try to have time every single day where the kids are outside playing and get them to do some activities instead of sitting them in front of the TV. Through repetition, what we are teaching our kids is very important. If every day it's just come home after school and it's TV time, and then I try once a week to break that habit and have them go outside, they wouldn't want anything to do with it.

So what we try to do is make the habit, the norm, which we want them to exemplify in their life, to get outside and play. When they come home from school, the first thing that we do is we send them outside to get some activity in beyond what they may have gotten at recess or something. Then, after dinner, they have some wind-down time, and they can enjoy a show that they like to watch. We try to keep TV until after dinner.

I think it is important to teach kids to be active early. At least sixty minutes a day. Again, I feel like when I was a kid we played for hours outside on a regular basis, and then on the weekends it was like we went outside in the morning and didn't come home until night. So we try to re-create some of the positive experiences we had as kids even though we live in a different day and age. We want our kids to be active and healthy.

The second part of that is nutrition. We focused on getting our kids to eat healthy early on as well. When we go out to eat, if our kids get into a habit of ordering off the kids menu and always eat chicken tenders, pizza, or mac and cheese, then that habit will be hard to break later on. When we go out to eat as a family, our kids eat the same type of meal off the menu that my wife and I eat.

Curtis Martin

HEALTH AND WELLNESS COACH

MY WIFE IS A CANCER survivor, and out of the battle with cancer and the recovery, my wife and I have both gone on a journey of fitness and health. We are both coaches now.

For me the key to cracking the nut with fitness and health was consistency. Getting healthy and fit is not a short-term fix, it is not a diet like we heard back in the day—the Atkins diet or today the keto diet or whatever the flavor of the week is. Honestly it comes down to consistency. For me with the busy work schedule that I had, ten to twelve hours a day, by the time you get home you're burned out, you're tired mentally and physically exhausted. For me the key was moving the exercise portion to the morning. I would set the alarm clock for four thirty each morning to get up and get that workout in first thing in the morning so that it is done. This way I don't have an excuse at seven or eight in the evening; I would just get up and get it done. It was a pre-stress relief because I knew what kind of day I was going in to was going to be hard.

My staff would joke with me at the time during our morning huddle, and they would know the days that I didn't work out. I would be drained and lack energy. But the days I did work out would be like I drank ten cups of coffee: I was perky.

So for me, the number one key is consistency. Just showing up every day. And I can take that same statement and carry it over into my aspects as a husband and a father. The best thing I can do for my wife and children is show up every day in their lives in the smallest ways or the biggest ways. Consistency is key.

Michael Morelli

PERSONAL TRAINER, FOUNDER OF MORELLIFIT

I KNOW WHAT IT IS like to beat addiction. It is fierce. It is challenging and the hardest thing I ever did. Cocaine had a hold on me, and I loved it. I think about those ten or twelve years, whatever it was, in total destruction, and I love sharing that because I believe through our vulnerability and these conversations we are healing more.

I drew a line in the sand—after feeling like total dogshit and learning that I was going to be a father—I drew a line in the sand, and over 113 days, through the internet and sifting through information and piecing things together, I lost about 27 pounds. I went from 185 pounds down to 147 pounds, and I saw my abs for the first time in my life. That was the thing where I realized that I could actually do this.

So from that point on, over a period of six months, I went and got six different certifications in the health and wellness space. I started a YouTube channel, and I stayed consistent, and through that consistency I wrote a bestselling book called *The Sweet Potato Diet*. We've sold over three hundred thousand programs in the wellness space collectively. Products, programs, we've got four brands. We're helping hundreds of thousands of people a year, if not millions, through a lot of our regular content. So now, as a result of this growing and this healing, my kids get to see me share my story and help hundreds of thousands of others.

I was the poor little depressed boy seven years ago who didn't think he could, just like a lot of people who don't think they can. If I can do it, anyone can do it. I'm not special. I didn't come down with any superpowers. I just did the work because of something pivotal that happened in my life: becoming a father.

Jeff Nichols

NAVY SEAL VETERAN

WE HAVE TO UNDERSTAND THAT when it comes to health, emotional health and physical health, those are all subjective components. Love, patience, kindness, and creativity are all subjective. Subjective behavior is considered to be a vulnerability, and vulnerability is considered to be weak. I think that we have to be okay with making mistakes and saying, "Hey, I made a mistake." It seems to me that we are at a place where if someone changes their mind then they're a hypocrite. I say no. I changed my mind and that's growth, not hypocrisy. But if you are constantly changing your mind, yes, that is hypocrisy.

You have to understand if you look at sports, and what is seen in the media, it's the home runs, the touchdowns, and catastrophes. It's the crescendos and the climaxes of life. But that's not how we develop these things. How do we learn to walk? We do it in a very safe manner with our parents around us facilitating that walking. That's with learning anything. Like math: you don't start with calculus, you start with basic mathematics.

To get to the end state, whether that's a pro ballplayer or a Navy SEAL, that is a process. We have basically underemphasized the necessity of a great process because the focal point is the end state. I put a lot of focus on the process and not the end state. Using BUD/S as an example, it's a guarantee that some of the people who show up to that course will graduate, and that process of BUD/S will create a SEAL. You don't just snap your fingers. There's a long process even before that to physically prepare. You have to formulate a process and stop looking at the end state.

Jordan Palmer

NFL VETERAN QUARTERBACK

WHEN IT COMES TO DECIDING whether or not to let your kids play tackle football, I sit uniquely in this because I've had concussions. I know exactly how many I had in college, and I know how many concussions I had in the NFL because it was well documented, and I had experts standing around me. What I don't know is how many I had when I was little. I started playing in third grade and nobody on the field was really qualified.

I think, as for today, the appropriate age to start playing tackle football is eighth grade or seventh grade on the early end. There are so many other ways to get good at football right now, particularly if they are a skill position—quarterback, running back, receiver, tight end, safety, corner, and linebacker. There are so many ways to get better. Seven-on-seven leagues are awesome. Kids can get a ton of development, a ton of skills without the need to run around and hit people. But I do think it is a good idea to get a year or two under your belt before you get to high school, learning how to hit but also learning how to be hit and how to protect yourself.

I would encourage any dads considering letting their sons play tackle football to look into Vicis helmets. Today if you're playing in the NFL, you could be using the same helmet you wore in middle school. That helmet is still available. If I wanted to wear the same cleats that I wore in middle school, I can't, because they don't make them anymore. There have been so many improvements to cleats that you can't get the old ones because they're so crappy, yet I can still wear the same helmet. Vicis has completly redesigned the helmet. When people ask me if my kids are going to play football, I say Dave Marver, the founder of Vicis, holds the keys to that answer. If the helmets do not improve by the time my son gets to high school, I would hope that he doesn't want to play football. If these helmets continue to improve, I would have much fewer concerns about a traumatic brain injury to my son.

Chris Powell

HOST OF *EXTREME WEIGHT LOSS*,
NEW YORK TIMES BESTSELLING AUTHOR

LOSING WEIGHT CAN BE A STRUGGLE for many dads out there, especially those who are working multiple jobs, coaching their kids in sports, and running around all the time who use the excuse of having limited time to commit to losing weight. So for all the dads out there who are slammed, know that you are not alone. Join the club.

It is absolutely crazy how busy our lives can get. You have to get in what you can when you can, and less is more. You see a lot of these programs that require you to go to the gym for an hour or an hour and a half, and right now that is just not a reality in my life. And I know it is like that for millions of dads out there. What you can do is what you can do. If that makes sense.

So I will literally carve out ten or fifteen minutes and do five pull-ups, ten push-ups, fifteen air squats, and I would do as many rounds of that as I can in ten minutes or fifteen minutes. That's all you gotta do. You're hitting every major muscle in the body. You're pushing, you're pulling, you're squatting, and when you are doing that multiple times for as many rounds as you can in ten or fifteen minutes, that's a monster workout. You're stimulating so many different muscles in the body, and when you do that there is a massive cardiovascular response.

If you have access to a stationary bike in your garage or if your apartment complex has a little fitness center, you can do ten minutes on the bike or do sprints. Do thirty seconds high intensity and thirty seconds low intensity for ten minutes. You will push a ton of oxygen into your system. So you're getting everything you need out of that. That is an intense workout session. The results are tenfold.

A lot of people think they have to carve out forty-five minutes or an hour for a workout. You really don't. I can assure you ten to fifteen minutes a day or sometimes even just five minutes is not just gonna reflect on your health. That sense of accomplishment is going to affect the way you treat other people and the way that you treat your family. So I don't just do it for my benefit; I do it for the benefit of my wife and kids as well.

Scott Reid

TWO-TIME BRITAIN'S STRONGEST MAN

WHEN I FINISHED COMPETING IN Strong Man, it was exceptionally taxing on my body. I was pushing, pushing, pushing, eating seven thousand–plus calories a day, most of it good food. My body hit a wall, and I ended up with chronic fatigue. The standard health-care system really doesn't have any answer for that, so I went back to basics. I did an elimination diet and started eating Paleo, strict Paleo, vegetables, good fats, organic meat.

From there I looked around to see what supplements could help. I found a group of supplements called adaptogens: codonopsis, rhodiola, reishi mushrooms, ashwagandha, and stuff like that. I kind of put together my own formula and networked with a guy who is a specialist in this field to use the supplements that were right for me. This, along with the Paleo diet, helped to cure my chronic fatigue.

So I highly recommend using some adaptogens. Ashwagandha helps regulate stress hormones and also helps to optimize testosterone levels within normal ranges and level cholesterol as well. Codonopsis gives you extra energy and helps you with cardiovascular health. So, if you are not training and you can't get in the gym every day, something like that is going to help you with health and longevity moving forward rather than just sticking some whey protein in your body, which you are not going to use and you won't need.

Michael Salzhauer

PLASTIC SURGEON KNOWN AS DR. MIAMI

IT'S ALL PSYCHOLOGICAL. What I do is psychology with a knife. The whole purpose is to make people feel better about their bodies so they can kind of get over it and have confidence and go on to do the things that they want to do.

If you don't feel good about yourself, it does limit your beliefs, and it limits your options in life. It can affect what kind of jobs you apply for, whom you marry, how you speak to other people, whether you make eye contact or not—all of those things carry over into every aspect.

Although what I do is surgery, the real change happens on the inside. Ninety-five percent of my clients are moms. Ninety-five percent are young mothers usually right after they are done having kids. I do tummy tucks, breast lifts, breast implants, Brazilian butt lifts, body reshaping, trying to get them back to where they were before they had kids or even better if possible.

A very common and mistaken male reaction from dads whose wives choose to have this work done is that they are trying to look good to attract other men. They think it's all about them. But it is really not about the men at all. It is just about the women feeling good in their own skin. If she doesn't feel good in her own skin, that can affect the marital relationship in the bedroom and in her life in general. A happy wife is a happy life. So when men come in and they ask me those questions, if this is a sign that something is wrong, I say no, but if it makes her happy it will make you happy. If your wife or girlfriend chooses to do this for herself, I would tell the husband, don't overthink it. It will benefit you in the end.

Aaron Singerman

BODYBUILDER, CEO OF REDCON1

WHEN I WAS A KID, it was pretty controversial that I was lifting weights at thirteen. My mom and dad had to come in and sign a gym membership and say that it was okay for me to go in there. I think these days the science has changed because back then people would be like, if you squat or lift heavy weights you won't get taller or your bones won't grow. I'm six foot three, and that's obviously not the case and science has proven that's not the case.

That being said, I wouldn't have a kid begin lifting weights before puberty. Push-ups, sit-ups, pull-ups, lunges, and air squats with no weights are okay. Body weight stuff will always be okay. You can do dips and all of that stuff. Your body, even as a child, is meant to be able to support your own weight without injury.

Now if you put 135 pounds on their back to squat, even if they can do it, that may cause some damage. But when you're a teenager, I think the real risk is if they are doing it wrong or if they are going too heavy. Kids will push the limits. I never ever considered getting injured or hurting or dying or any of that when I was a kid. So I pushed it much harder than I would advise my son to. If my son wants to lift weights when he is thirteen, I will 100 percent encourage him to deadlift, bench, squat, and I will teach him the right form so he doesn't hurt himself.

Steve Weatherford

NFL VETERAN PUNTER, SUPER BOWL CHAMPION,
NFL'S FITTEST MAN

I HAVE BEEN SO FORTUNATE to have experienced so many rad things in my life. I can speak from a lifetime of experience of being in some really dark places and being addicted to drugs or having marital problems or second-guessing my purpose on Earth, dealing with depression and dealing with anxiety, through all of this craziness—also winning the Super Bowl. It's so easy for us to look at people's resumes and people's Instagram pages and just assume that their life is amazing. But I was dealing with some really dark things for a really long time.

At a young age I was always very challenged by adversity, and I think that had a lot to do with my very low self-worth. I felt like I needed to achieve and accomplish in order to be worthy of love and worthy of people caring about me. I was sexually abused when I was in seventh grade; then having to move from Baton Rouge, Louisiana, to Terre Haute and be the new kid, the skinny kid and always carrying around the guilt of what happened.

It's been a wild journey, but looking back on my life, that all happened for me and allowed me to be in the place I am right now. I think it all has to do with how you interpret it. You can look at life as happening to you or life happening for you—and that's life in general. When one opportunity seems to be taken away from you, that really just means there's another opportunity that is better suited for you. And if you can look at life that way from a perspective of life is happening for me versus to me, it really turns obstacles into opportunities.

Robb Wolf

RESEARCH BIOCHEMIST, HEALTH EXPERT,
AUTHOR OF *THE PALEO SOLUTION*

IT'S GOOD BIOLOGY AND WIRING for kids to want to eat all the snacky, refined foods. In the past, that would've been a real boon, but in our modern day where kids barely get any physical activity—I mean they go to a soccer match that lasts twenty-five minutes, and then they're deluged with cupcakes and Gatorade afterwards when the kids have barely even broken a sweat. None of that stuff is serving us all that well.

We never use food as a reward system. I don't even call it treats; it's still just food. There are certain consequences to the food that we have access to, and I'm trying to make my two girls aware of those nuances while also acknowledging the way that human beings are wired up. We never really keep much junk food in the house. Kids become picky eaters mainly because they have either super delicious junk food options, which they naturally, not surprisingly, gravitate toward, or you feed them mainly un-processed foods.

You have to set the benchmark early. In our house, we have a little bit of ice cream once in a while. There are actually some low-carb ice creams that are really good. We grab some sorbet for the girls occasionally, but we kind of do a speed bump method where they have to eat their protein, they have to eat their veggies, they have to eat some real food, and then maybe at the end of that process, they can have something like some ice cream.

I know this stuff just gets people angry and riled up, but from my perspective it's kind of like the discipline deal, where parents can either choose to let the inmates run the asylum or you set the pacing on this stuff. I talk with my girls about my work, and my work is involved with trying to help avert the catastrophe we're all facing with type 2 diabetes, obesity, and neurodegenerative disease. So I am very honest with them. When people eat poorly, they tend to not feel well, they tend to get sick, they could die early, and I just try to explain that stuff. We talk about how if we mainly focus on the front end of meals with a focus on whole good foods, then we can have a little bit of the other stuff and kick our heals up.

Finance
and Education

"**C**AN I AFFORD to start a family?" This is a top question on the minds of most men before they have their first child. We're constantly told how expensive it is to have a child. Some men will even have a magic milestone they must reach before they'll consider bringing another life into this world. Establishing a career, eliminating debt, and buying a house are among the most common requirements for many guys.

What's interesting is that the average size of a new single-family home in the United States is 2,531 square feet. The average household size is 2.63 people. This is in contrast to a hundred years ago, in the 1920s, when the average size of a new single-family home was 750 square feet, and the average household size was 4.34. A hundred years ago, it also was common for married couples to have six or more children, while today that's relatively unheard of. As our homes have gotten bigger, our families have gotten smaller.

One of the major causes of financial concerns, especially debt, is college tuition. If you're still paying off your college loans, the thought of saving for a child to go to college can be daunting. What's even worse is that according to a Gallup poll conducted in 2019, a staggering 85 percent of people hate their jobs. Far too many people are working in fields that are much different than what they attended college for and don't require the degree they're still paying off.

The rise of technology has opened the door to endless opportunities, especially for entrepreneurs and side hustlers. For years, I drove a metered cab as a part-time job, and now my smartphone allows me to drive for Uber and Lyft. I can create my own hours and drive when and where I choose.

Also, using my iPhone, I created my podcast, *First Class Fatherhood*. I have yet to use any other device to record, edit, and publish my show. With only a smartphone, you can create a website and open your own online store within minutes. So, in the words of Jim Rohn, if you're working a job that you hate and would love to pursue other interests, "Work full time on your job and part time on your fortune."

The first thing you need to do is get the knowledge and then apply it with action. The first part is easy, thanks to the technology available at our fingertips. The second part, taking action, will determine the results. On my podcast, I've had the honor of speaking with many successful entrepreneur dads. Some, such as Ed Mylett and Joel Marion, went from being broke to being worth millions. Success leaves clues, and all of these guys drop valuable nuggets of information for free on their social media pages. One question I love to ask entrepreneur dads is, "Is college necessary for kids to succeed in today's world?"

Teaching kids financial literacy—what to do with a dollar, how to invest, how to set goals, how to save money, and a lot of other important information—should be introduced to kids in grammar school and continued through high school. Unfortunately, that's typically not done. One book I highly recommend for teenagers is *The Richest Man in Babylon* by George S. Clason, which dispenses financial advice through parables that young readers can easily decipher. The younger children start learning about finances, the greater the chance they can avoid a financial calamity later in life.

Whenever I hear young men say it's too expensive to have kids, I reply, "If you think kids cost too much money, then wait until you're over sixty years old, and life hits you with the bill for not having any." Yes, kids cost a lot of money, but for the many men I know who are over sixty who never had any, the price of childlessness is often much higher.

You're about to read some of the best advice given by entrepreneurs, businessmen, a professor of financial literacy, and others who answered questions about how to switch careers and start your own business, how to teach your kids about money, whether sending your kids to college is necessary, and all things related to finance and education.

Edwin Arroyave

FOUNDER AND CEO OF SKYLINE SECURITY MANAGEMENT

I GRADUATED WITH A 1.8 GPA and didn't go to college. I would say college is great as far as the associations that you can build in college. You are going to meet people that are going to stretch you, and in life you have to be stretched. If you hang out with the right people you are probably going to do pretty well, so I think college is great for that. College is great for teaching you how to start something and finish it. It helps you to build identity.

But I believe the most important thing is to develop your mindset and principles of success. Those are the things that will take you to the next level. There are a lot of guys who have college degrees, but their mindset isn't right. In a perfect world you have mindset and education together, but if I had to choose one, I would go mindset all day. I would go with learning the principles of personal development all day long.

One of my biggest fears that I suppressed for many years was I didn't think I was very smart. The reason I didn't think I was very smart is because the school system made me believe that because I didn't get good grades and because I couldn't pass tests that I wasn't smart. So I had that deep down in my unconscious mind, and for many years I would suppress it by telling myself as long as I work harder than people, as long as I have discipline, integrity, faith, and perseverance then I would eventually beat people out.

That worked for twenty-one years until I surpassed what I thought I was worth. The company was worth $40 million, and I began to have all these doubts that I wasn't smart enough. And when that happens, you start to self-sabotage. You will self-sabotage to bring yourself back down to what you think you're worth. The company and I started to go in a downward spiral, and it wasn't until I began studying personal development and learning from guys like Grant Cardone and Ed Mylett that everything changed. Through studying personal development, my biggest fear has now become my biggest gift back to the world. And the way you make a positive impact is by sharing your gifts with the world and helping others do the same.

Audie Attar

FOUNDER AND CEO OF PARADIGM SPORTS MANAGEMENT

I ENCOURAGE EVERY DAD TO follow their dreams. At the end of the day, we live in the greatest country in the world. We have the ability to do anything we want so long as you get up off your butt and go do it.

If you are a dad who is stuck working in a job that you hate and are looking to make a change, and maybe are thinking of going the entrepreneur route, the first thing I would say is you are going to have to learn to be comfortable in uncomfortable situations. You have to understand that nothing great happens overnight. It takes time. Follow your passion, follow your dreams, but make sure you do enough research and prepare and don't just jump into something blindly.

Even if you follow your dreams, it is going to be difficult. There's going to be many sleepless nights. There are going to be times where you have to figure out how to buy diapers and put food on the table. As an entrepreneur you are cutting everyone else's check before you write yourself a check. Ultimately you have to be ready to be uncomfortable like that, and more importantly, you should plan accordingly. That plan should not only prepare you for very turbulent times but, more importantly, should make it so you understand when it's time to pivot and go in a different direction with that endeavor or your personal career.

Jordan Belfort

THE WOLF OF WALL STREET

I DON'T THINK COLLEGE IS necessary to succeed in today's world. I think college is a total scam. With that being said, if somebody wants to be a doctor, lawyer, or engineer, there are certain very definable careers that need formal training.

But I would say outside that 5 or 10 percent of people, it's the biggest waste of time and scam in the world. All they do is indoctrinate people to an ultraliberal way of thinking and turn them into soft marshmallows. It's also a monetary scam because they pump up the price of college by allowing people to borrow massive amounts of money, which leaves people straddled with student debt, and they have no skill set to then pay back that money. It's a total scam, college.

Think and Grow Rich was the first book that I read that opened my eyes to a lot of things that I was already doing. I was born with a certain mindset and way of thinking. I think everybody has their own sort of generic disposition, and mine was very much weighted toward entrepreneurship. For parents who have younger kids, I think it's up to you to really empower your kids so they know they have control over their lives and their happiness. They have to take ownership and not have the type of thinking that the world happens to them but that they are the ones who dictate what happens in the world around them, that through their actions they can make a difference. I think that's one of the most important things you can instill in your kids outside of unconditional love.

Grant Cardone

CEO OF CARDONE ENTERPRISES, CARDONE CAPITAL,
FOUNDER OF 10X MOVEMENT

MY DAD DIED WHEN HE was fifty-two years old, and that impacted me and was so crucial in my life, because in that moment I realized that people die, and they leave their family. So since then, I began looking for that vehicle that will not leave my wife and my kids in the same predicament my dad did. My dad was a hard worker and a good person, but no matter how hard you work and how nice of a person you are, when you die and the money stops, you die and the money stops.

I want dads to know that real estate is the thing that can live hundreds of years beyond you. My first deal was a single unit, and I wouldn't do that again, and I would advise anyone not to buy a single unit. My next deal was for thirty-two units, and those thirty-two units, if I still owned them today, would be enough to support my wife and kids for the rest of their lives. I now own over five thousand units, so that will certainly provide for them.

I would tell dads about how to make the jump from working a job to getting into real estate is don't make the jump. It's not about making a jump. I didn't make a jump. What I did was, while I was doing my main job, on the weekends and at night, all I would do was look at real estate. I continued to work hard so I didn't lose my income stream, but with all of my free time I shopped real estate, looked at it, and learned about it. Any free money I had was being stored and accumulated so that one day I could buy a deal.

Evan Carmichael

ENTREPRENEUR AND YOUTUBER

THE BEST THING YOU CAN DO with your kids is, as soon as they get an idea for something, have them go and try it. Teach them to go from idea to attempt and just get started. If they want to be YouTubers, then help them make their first YouTube video. You may have no idea what you are doing and that's fine, because neither do they. Get your phone out and make the first video and have them figure out how to download an app to edit the video and post it up.

If you are under thirteen, you can't have your own YouTube channel legally, so the parent has to have the account, and you are going to want to monitor what they are posting up anyway. But I think that is a fun project to do together.

If your kids are interested in the stars, then maybe this weekend you go out of town where there are no lights and you look at the stars and now they are learning about the Big Dipper and the constellations.

I think the more you can encourage your kids to go off and explore their interests, that's how they are going to find their passion. I think people get lost into careers too soon, and they do things because their parents did them or they are expected to get into those careers. I think that is why most people are unhappy. Ninety-five percent of America wakes up and goes to a job that they don't like. If you want your kids to be happy, it starts with figuring out what their passions are, and the sooner you do that, the better.

One of the greatest things about having kids is that you get to learn about a whole bunch of things you never knew about before as they pull you into it. Use that as the strength of your relationship with your kids instead of sighing and saying, "Oh great! Now I have to learn YouTube." Take that as a chance to connect with your kids and learn some new skills together.

Andy Dane Carter

REAL ESTATE EXPERT, AUTHOR, PODCASTER

HERE IS WHAT I TELL EVERYBODY, and some people don't like it. But it is just my truth. Do not buy a house. Do not, as your first piece of real estate, buy a house. When you buy a house, it is owned by the bank. It is an asset that is owned by the bank. Most kids coming out of high school and college want to buy a house; they have a car that's leased, they have some credit card debt, and student loan debt. That puts them in a very interesting head space for a long time.

My suggestion is to buy a duplex, a triplex, or a fourplex instead of a house. Let's say you buy a fourplex, and it has a little front house with three units in the back, which you can rent out. You can put 3.5 percent down, so on a $700,000 fourplex, $24,000 gets you into that property. Now you can become a landlord, live in one of the units, rent out the other units to cover 80 percent or 100 percent of the mortgage, and now you are creating wealth, generational wealth.

If you or your kids are twenty-two years old and not sure what you want to do and don't want to buy something so you're stuck somewhere, then buy a fourplex. Live in one of the units, then go travel the world and rent out your unit using Airbnb to pay for your travel. There are so many possibilities when it comes to real estate and creating wealth.

Kent Clothier

CEO OF REAL ESTATE WORLDWIDE

AS LONG AS YOU ARE trapped by your perceptions—"It takes money to make money" and all the little nuances and information we feed ourselves—that quickly becomes what we believe, and therefore we don't take action. I can tell you that if you believe there is an opportunity inside of real estate, and you believe that you want to control your time to have freedom to spend more time with your family, to do the things that actually matter and not run around and make somebody else rich, then you absolutely owe it to yourself to get educated. That's the first step. Get the information, and then the next step is to take action.

Do things that are very uncomfortable the first time you do them, just like anything else in your life. But do them and then repeat them. Repetition is the mother of retention, as the saying goes. If you keep doing these things over and over, suddenly you have this new skill set that not only can replace any income that you have right now but ultimately exceed it wildly. The first step is to go get the education. You could follow someone like me online, or there are plenty of other people, but information is right at your fingertips. Whether that's YouTube videos, online courses, or books, get the real data before making a mistake by telling yourself this is not possible.

Brandon Copeland

PROFESSOR OF FINANCIAL LITERACY, NFL LINEBACKER

FINANCIAL LITERACY SHOULD BE TAUGHT in high schools and even before that. It is the one class that we all will use no matter what our major is or what our profession is, because you need your credit if you want to buy a car or a house one day. We should talk about these things before doing them. The things I am going to teach my son initially—besides setting him up with a 529, if you can afford to, which will make things easier for him and yourself later on—I want to teach him the value of a dollar. So he understands when he gets a dollar how to save it and appreciate it. I think, with children, they don't see the why or the how things are being bought. They don't know the cost behind it and that is our job as parents for them to be protected from "real-world thoughts."

However, I want him to appreciate it so, as he gets older, he doesn't have the philosophy of spending every dollar he makes. I want him to be thinking that when he gets a dollar, he's splitting it into save, spend, and share jars. With that, it would be thirty-three cents is to save, thirty-three cents is to spend, and thirty-three cents is to give to a cause or something. I just want to get that ingrained in him. That way he really understands how to save.

The number one thing is that it is not what you make, it is what you spend. I know it sounds easy for me to say that on an NFL salary, but there's a reason why people hit the lottery and go broke. It's not what you make, it's what you spend and how you spend it and adjusting the budget and all of those different things.

Eli Crane

NAVY SEAL VETERAN, FOUNDER OF BOTTLE BREACHER

I LOVE THE SIDE HUSTLE. Any dad who is working a job out there that he hates, I would encourage them to do what I did and start a side hustle at night and on weekends. It might mean that you don't get to watch your favorite episode of *Survivor* or whatever your show happens to be. It might mean that you don't get to hang out with your friends on the weekend. But one of my favorite sayings is, "Entrepreneurs are willing to work like nobody is willing to work so they can live lives that nobody is able to live!" There is a lot of truth to that statement.

If you start a side hustle at nights and on weekends, when most of your friends are hanging out, sleeping, or whatever else they are doing, yet you are still paying your bills during the day with your regular job, that's a really great way to start. Most of us don't have a rich mom and dad or a trust fund or an investor that's willing to throw money at us right off the bat. I'm a firm believer that to win at life you have to swing for the fences. And sometimes you have to go big and at times you have to put yourself outside your comfort zone. There's a lot more failure than most people ever really know.

I also believe that the most successful people in life don't look at failure the same way that everybody else does. They just look at it as that's where the lessons are learned. I try to fail faster and acquire more knowledge and more lessons learned so that when I get the opportunity for another attempt, I don't make the same mistakes.

Jesse Csincsak

PROFESSIONAL SNOWBOARDER, ENTREPRENEUR,
WINNER OF *THE BACHELORETTE*

I SAW MY DAD WORKING crazy hours driving a semitruck making pennies, working for the man. I got that work ethic from him. Both my mom and my dad worked their fingers to the bone. I watched my dad, who was always working and never home, and I thought there has to be more to life than this.

I got a paper route when I was ten years old, and it showed me that I got out of it what I put in. Some local entrepreneurs took me under their wings while I was growing up, and I liked that lifestyle much better. The idea of being your own boss is far better than working for someone else and being at the mercy of them deciding to fire you.

My kids want to start a YouTube channel, and I am not opposed to it. I know there are many young people making a lot of money online and on YouTube. I am a believer in the old-school way of using your hands and teaching my kids the old industrial way Americans made a living, because the jobs available with those skill sets are recession proof. Jobs like auto mechanics, diesel mechanics, plumbers, landscapers, all those jobs where people work with their hands, it doesn't matter if we go into another recession, those jobs aren't going away. Your homeowners' association is still going to hit you with a fine if you don't trim your trees and pull your weeds.

I know we live in an age of computers, but we are also one dirty bomb away from going back to living in the stone age life of a hundred years ago. So, yes, we have computers, and my kids are learning on computers, but I think it is so important to teach my kids how to start a fire, how to chop firewood, how to run a chainsaw. I think that is an important part of education as well.

Kyren Gibson

YOUTUBER, INFLUENCER

I MADE THE VIDEOS THAT went viral with my son and me talking about finances and investing for a couple of reasons. I am trying to end this mindset of "Black men don't take care of their kids"; so that's number one. We do; we are here. Let's start talking about the positive and stop talking about the negative.

Secondly, I'm trying to inspire all dads to be involved with their kids. We can't depend on the school system to teach them everything. As a parent, we can't just keep giving our kids money and telling them to go to the mall. Being a parent is more in depth than that, and I'm just trying to show everybody.

Kids will learn if you will teach them and open their minds. My son always asks to play video games, but I tell him he has to study first because it is his studies that will enable him to support a family someday.

There's a million ways you can be successful and take care of your family; it's not just music and sports. That was my problem. I was lost. A lot of athletes can go broke because they don't know what to do. Too many people depend on "I'm gonna make it," but when you don't make it, what are you going to do now? Everyone loves sports and music, but you have to be realistic with yourself. Somebody is going to have an injury. Everybody has a story, and a lot of people are going to have that story of they didn't make it. I want my son and other kids to know that you have to expand your brain early so you can find other ways of succeeding. So you have to be open-minded with them.

Tyler Jack Harris

SOLD EIGHT THOUSAND LIFE INSURANCE POLICIES
IN THREE AND A HALF YEARS

IF YOU ARE UNEMPLOYED RIGHT now or you are employed in a career that you just don't feel is right for you, then you can do something about that. You have the ability to make that change. When you take full ownership and understand that everything is your fault, you break free of the handcuffs. You basically take the key back from everyone else that you have been putting the blame on, and you allow yourself to break free. The encouragement and understanding of that is that you realize, "Hey, if I got myself into this, then I can get myself out of it."

I think a lot of us are still playing this blame game, which I did for several years, saying, "My wife did this," or "My former employer did that." As long as you keep pointing your fingers outward, you're going to get nowhere. Once you point those fingers back toward you is when you can actually take steps to get yourself out of the situation that you are in.

The most successful people I know are the most patient people. I think many fathers are in a place right now where they feel like they have made some bad decisions and now they have to make up for time lost, they have to recover from all the time they have spent in the wrong career. They start making decisions with a lack of patience, and the decisions ultimately become too risky or lead them down the wrong path. The important thing to know is that you can make a change today. It may take a few years, but as long as you are doing the right thing compounded over time, it is going to lead you where you want to go. But it all starts with taking ownership and putting the blame on yourself.

Bedros Keuilian

FOUNDER AND CEO OF FIT BODY BOOT CAMP

WHEN IT COMES TO EDUCATION and sending their kids to school, most parents just go, "Hey, I did this, so you have to go through this pain too." When the parents don't know any alternative, they say, do what I did: Go get good grades, go to school, you're going to accumulate college debt, then go work for a company that's going to keep you around. You can work your way up the food chain, and over time you might retire with a pension and a gold watch.

Well, those days are gone. What parents should be saying is, "The way I did it was wrong," or "The way I did it was right for that time." Today we live in a new economy, yet the parents are too stubborn to take their head out of the sand and look around and realize that if you have the solution to a problem, the internet will help you spread that solution virally, quickly, force multiply, time collapse, and for that to happen parents need to read books like my book *Man Up*. They need to understand they can be on the exponential growth financially and not the linear growth of maybe getting a 1.5–3 percent increase in pay every year, which most of the time doesn't even cover the cost of inflation.

I'm teaching my kids to use YouTube and watch what other kids are doing, kids who are their age and entrepreneurial. I take them out of school and bring them to speaking events with me so they can learn from successful people.

Parents need to use the resources they have, and the internet has great information. If you want your kids to have the best shake at life, they should be following people like me, like Gary Vaynerchuck, Ed Mylett, and Tom Billout because there is so much great content that is free.

College is not the way unless you specifically want to be a doctor, engineer, architect, accountant, or an attorney. Outside of that, if you are just going to be a bean counter for someone, there is probably something better you can be doing that will give you more meaning, a greater sense of satisfaction, greater control over your life and time, and of course more money. Way more money than you can ever make counting beans for someone else.

Brad Lea

FOUNDER AND CEO OF LIGHTSPEED VT

MANY DADS ARE WORKING IN jobs that they hate and are afraid to make a change because it might cause financial difficulty for their families. I was in that position, and I feared more that I would never be able to provide more and be the dad I wanted to be and be able to afford the things I wanted to afford for my children.

Ultimately, I had to take a chance because I feared more staying the same than I did failing. I mean, the worst-case scenario, you go get a job. Worst-case scenario if things don't work out quickly, you can go back and get the same job or a similar job to the one you had. Jobs are a dime a dozen. Opportunities are everywhere.

If you feel like you are not in the position you want to be and you can't be the father that you want to be or the provider that you want to be and you are stuck in a job, it's an excuse. "I have kids to support so I can't afford to take a chance." Well, I would reverse that. I would say, "I have kids so I cannot afford not to."

I think the biggest mistakes most entrepreneurs have at the beginning is not thinking big enough. Most people underestimate how long it will take, they underestimate how much it will take, how much work it is, and they don't think big enough. Their goals are not big enough.

If you are a parent that is working a job that you love but are having trouble inspiring or instilling aspirational goals in your kids—sometimes parents aren't looked at as the experts by their kids—the best thing that I've found is to try and identify those thought leaders and influencers that you align with and accidentally introduce them to your kids. Sometimes you cannot get through to a kid and get them to understand the logic of things. So a good way to do that would be to enlist the help of other influencers. Try to find a new voice they will listen to rather than your own.

Sean Matson

NAVY SEAL, CEO OF MATBOCK,

CEO OF CARDOMAX, CEO OF DECON PRODUCTS

FOR ANY DAD OUT THERE, especially a veteran dad who is thinking about starting their own business, my advice is to just do it! Don't be afraid of it. If you are a veteran, then a lot of things you learned in the military apply to the business world; it is just a different language. If you look at it this way, then your business plan is a five-paragraph OPORD (Situation, Mission, Execution, Sustainment, and Command). That's a business plan, and you can break down the five-paragraph OPORD individually into details and tasks and start moving forward.

As a father, if your kids are younger than five and you are worried about missing time with them, it's not the time to worry. They probably aren't going to remember much. As they get older, they are going to start remembering things like dad wasn't there a lot. It is very stressful and very time consuming, but the flexibility that I have is tremendous. I am my own boss so if I want to go have lunch with my kids, I schedule it and I make it happen. So that is something I love to do.

I try to make every sporting event that they are at and basically work my travel around my time with them. There are some times when that doesn't work out, but the majority of the time that is my priority, and I am in the position to make that happen.

When your kids are at school or as soon as they go to sleep, that gives you plenty of time, which you can devote to the business. It's just really about time management, and you having to dedicate your time. I use different scheduling apps to help me with that process. One rule is when I am with my kids, I do not take conference calls. If I know I am going to be with my kids, I do not schedule any calls.

David Meltzer

COFOUNDER OF SPORTS 1 MARKETING

PROFITABILITY WITHOUT PASSION or purpose is an empty feeling. I see through athletes, entertainers, multimillionaires—so many empty people. I try to tell them to shift the paradigm of value.

We all should be appreciators. Appreciation has two sides to it. One is gratitude—that we should be grateful for everything we have in life. If you want to change your life, it's simple: just say thank you before you go to bed and when you wake up. Your whole life will change if you do that every day.

The second part of appreciation is to add value. I believe that most people don't have a problem with giving and being grateful; they really have a problem with receivership. They don't understand that you can't even know what you have until you've given it away. Our purpose or passion should be to take what we receive, add value to it, and give it away. That's the passion and purpose that I have.

I do a lot of business coaching, and one of the most common questions I get is, "How do I start a business when I have family obligations?" I tell people all the time that the legs feed the lion. So the first step, if you feel stuck at your current job and want to be an entrepreneur, is to be better at your job. Be more efficient and try to get paid more at your current job, because the better you are at your current job the more options or opportunities you will have to invest your time or money into starting a business.

What so many people end up doing is draining the legs and wondering why they can never start a business. And the job that they are at is making less and less money and taking more and more time. I challenge people to do their job better, be a professional, fuse what you are doing today with purpose, be the best that you can be, and try to do your job better and faster so you have more time and money to increase the options and opportunities for you to start your own business.

Shawn Nelson

FOUNDER AND CEO OF LOVESAC

I WOULD NEVER UNDERESTIMATE THE value of college—but go to learn. I think too many people just want to get through and want to party and have a good time. Play along the way, for sure, but go to learn and pick a subject or a major that you really want to throw yourself into and become some kind of expert in something. I think there will be value beyond that which you can predict going into it.

I don't think college is necessary to succeed in today's world, but I actually completed university and went on later in my thirties and did a master's just because I wanted to learn more. I think you should go to school to learn. There is an endless sea of information and knowledge out there and you should expose yourself to it.

If you have a good idea and want to start a business, my best advice is to get off the couch. For me, I was literally sitting on my parents' couch when I was eighteen watching *The Price Is Right* eating a bowl of Cap'n Crunch when I had this idea for a bean bag the size of the whole living room. I think the thing that really separated me from so many wantrepreneurs is I literally got off the couch right then, got in my car, drove down to Joann Fabrics, and bought supplies. I came home and started making the thing. I didn't have any idea it was going to become a business, and it took many years before it was a business. But just do something. It's one thing to think about it. It's another thing to make plans, and it's another thing to actually take steps and do stuff. It might shock you how far some of those simple steps can take you.

Chris Patterson

ENTREPRENEUR, OWNER OF INTERCHANGES

I THINK THE MOST IMPORTANT THING is to teach kids what money is and what it isn't. I'm not the sharpest tool in the shed often, so I look to lean on other people. Years ago we were broke, actually less than broke—we were over fifty thousand dollars in debt. I began studying Dave Ramsey's principles on Financial Peace University. He has a seven-step—baby steps—process of getting out of debt. I followed every one of the steps and now I'm on step seven, which is the highest you can get.

I turned back to my kids and decided to show them how to give, save, and spend. I showed them the value of work. I showed them the value of understanding that you are here for a purpose. You need to work hard to figure out what that purpose is and serve other people. The reason I believe we are all here on Earth is to serve one another. I think it all becomes defunct when we decide to just serve ourselves and ourselves only. It is just a matter of sitting down and taking the time to teach your kids the value of money and how to manage it.

I was mentored by Zig Ziglar, who introduced me to something called a performance planner. It helps me to set up my goals every year, and I manage those goals on a monthly basis, and then I drill that down to a daily basis of performance and consistency. The performance planner helps me day by day understand exactly where I am at and when I'm being lazy.

I used to be asked a lot while I was doing networking events, "What was the secret to your success?" I was tired of trying to answer that question in twenty different ways, so I took a picture of myself holding ten of these performance planners, each one representing one year. Now I just pull up that picture and say this is what I did. I keep track of what I'm supposed to be doing, set goals, and get aggressive toward hitting each one of those goals, and that has led me to financial success.

Bill Perkins

PROFESSIONAL POKER PLAYER, AUTHOR

I'VE BEEN SEEING SO MANY people not get the most out of their life. They are working, working, working, and that's great for survival. They get so good at working that they just keep working, and they die with a bunch of money.

I ask what were you saving for? The first thing people save for is survival and some variance in their life. I've noticed that those who are working and those who are saving save too much. They essentially delay gratification past the point where it's too late and there's no gratification. To me that is a waste. Why aren't they taking vacations with their families and their kids, going camping or going hunting? It can get very habitual when you're caught up in the rat race and not working for any kind of reward. People are paying or their insurance will pay hundreds of thousands of dollars for them to live an extra five days on their deathbed when they could've been having big family dinners, big family trips, and getting the most out of life.

I want people to lose the fear so they can optimize their life and lead the most fulfilling life they can, and the way people have fulfilling lives is by having experiences they want to have. Whether that's taking your family on a trip or helping other people in unfortunate situations. Experiences create your narrative. You have to take a step back and plan. You need to know how much you need to survive and what you are saving for. Get off the autopilot of work, work, work, and think about what you are working for. What experiences do you want to have and when do you want to have them?

Life has seasons, and there are certain experiences that go into those seasons. If you didn't go to Disney World and ride the Dumbo ride with your kids when they were younger, then you missed the boat on that. When they are eighteen, they aren't gonna ride the Dumbo ride with you. That's true with everything. You need to make sure that the list of experiences you want to have with your kids, that you put them in the right seasons. What I call the right time bucket.

Kilay Reinfeld

PARTNER AND PRESIDENT OF
PARADIGM SPORTS MANAGEMENT

WHETHER OR NOT COLLEGE IS necessary to succeed in today's world really depends on the person and their character. My wife couldn't have made it without going to school. She is a physiologist, she's a doctor, so she needed that degree to do what her passion was. I dropped out of high school in tenth grade. I got my GED and went to college for a year and dropped out of college as well because I couldn't stand it.

During that whole process, I had already started multiple businesses and I was making more money than most of my friends. But I am always learning. I am reading every day. I'm always diving into tech, and I've always had a big passion for learning on my own. I think that is the tough part with college. It's not for everyone, but anybody who is willing to learn can do that.

A lot of people ask me how to start a business, and I believe the hardest part of that is finding what you are passionate about. The most important part is to know what you want to do. The computer and the internet are tools. I remember back in the early '90s the philosophy was you put up a website and you just wait and all this stuff happens. Today it is a lot more focused and honed in to the idea of knowing what you want to do. And you have to do it the same way online that you would doing it retail. You have to put the time and effort into what you want and use the tools that are available as tools, not as some kind of magic wand that is just going to make it happen.

Matt Sapaula

UNITED STATES MARINE, MONEY SMART GUY

MY WIFE AND I ARE blessed to be cash-flow millionaires. We make seven figures a year, and we can literally afford to pay for any one of our kids' college tuition without them having any student loan debt. We suggested to our oldest three kids, who graduated high school, that if they are not going to study science, medicine, engineering, or become a lawyer, then go off into the business world. Go off and find a job. Go off and find out what the world can teach you, because the world is a harsh lesson in maturity. Go out there and get beat up a little and then come back and talk to me with your experience, and we can have a different relationship going forward.

So many kids are going to college, and they don't know what they want to do. In the beginning, I didn't have a passion for insurance, savings, and investment. It was just a career path for me. As

I continued to learn, grow, develop—and learn about the money game, learn how our economy works, learn about capitalism and entrepreneurship and how the political world can affect our financial lives—I started to understand how it all works.

A lot of people are so unaware of what is going on in their financial home let alone the political world and how that affects their pocketbooks. There's a bigger purpose behind it. You need to take control of your financial home; that way people can avoid a lot of arguments and conflict in the home. Therefore, they can become better dads, better family members, and do what they really want to do with their future.

Steve Sims

**AUTHOR, SPEAKER, COACH,
KNOWN AS THE REAL-LIFE WIZARD OF OZ**

ANY DAD WHO IS AN ENTREPRENEUR should take their kids to work or should have their kids listen in on their business calls. The schools are teaching stuff that we will never use, or there is an app that we could download that will do it faster. The world of an entrepreneur, the world of a businessperson, needs to be taught to kids, and it can only be taught in real life. So if they need to hear you on the phone closing a deal, lose a deal, try to rectify a deal, or try to solve a problem that was either your fault or not your fault—these are the things that you need to be teaching your kids.

I can say, by luck, I used to have my kids, at a young age, listen to my phone calls when I was in the car. It taught them how to negotiate, manage, respond, and take responsibility for when things go wrong. So parents should do that, for one thing.

Secondly, if you are paying your kids to do chores during the week—let's say you are paying them twenty dollars to do the weekly chores—at the end of the week, if they haven't done one of the chores, hold back five dollars. Or, worse, say, "Hey, I pay you five dollars to do that, and you didn't do it. So I had to do it, and my rate is higher than yours." So deduct ten dollars. They won't make that mistake again.

Ryan Stewman

THE HARDCORE CLOSER

MOST PEOPLE ARE NEVER FORCED out of a job, so they get into a comfortable situation to where they are living maybe beyond their means or right at their means. And that makes it impossible for them to go a month or two without a paycheck.

One of the best decisions I ever made, and it's never too late to make this decision: I always live way below my means. Even today, I live on probably 10 percent of my income. That's a lot easier for me to do these days because I'm a multimillionaire, but even when I was making $250,000 a year back in 2009, I was living in a $115,000 house that cost $600 a month to own.

I was never a person who was living on the level I was earning. For so many dads, they are already so far in debt and so far behind the curve that they can't see the outcome. There are guys out there like Dave Ramsey who can teach you how to eliminate debt. There are guys like John Cummuta who teach how to turn debt into wealth. There are programs you can get involved in that are cheap. You can watch YouTube videos on how to consolidate debt. If you are stuck in a job that you hate and you have a lot of debt, when you do finally consolidate it, don't go stack up more. Live below your means. Stop eating steak dinners and going out to the bars, because all of these things start to add up.

Troy Vincent

EXECUTIVE VICE PRESIDENT
OF NFL FOOTBALL OPERATIONS

WHEN IT COMES TO PARENTS selecting a college that is right for their student athlete, they should identify an institution that is the best fit for the child. In finding that culture, it is important to ask appropriate questions and have a plan. Resist the temptation to decal chase.

The one piece of advice I would give every parent is to be realistic. Have realistic expectations for your child, and don't decal chase. Don't put your child in a situation where he or she is going to an institution that just may be a little bit above where they should be playing to have fun. Have a list of questions that will help find the suitable culture based on how your child was raised. Remember, your child will spend most of their time, for example as football players, with their position coach. Who is he? What is he about? Look at some of the other athletes that he has coached. Where are they in life? What is the graduation rate? What is campus life like? Is there a balance of being a student and a student athlete on campus? How are the athletes perceived on campus? Do the young men or women that your son or daughter will be engaged with, do they share similar values?

All of those questions are important, because the last thing you want to do is send your child to an institution and they end up hurting, unhappy. You'll be getting a phone call late at night, and you will now be asking the coach, "Why isn't my child playing?" So on and so forth. In making that choice with your student athlete, don't daddy ball, don't decal chase, and really have a plan in finding the right institution, the right culture for your child.

Colin Wayne

FOUNDER AND CEO OF REDLINE STEEL

I'M NOT AGAINST EDUCATION or going to college. That is ultimately up to you. But I don't think that you need it to be successful. I feel very confident in my marketability and my go-to market strategies that I could run circles around other people with PhDs. Don't let your lack of higher education limit your mindset of "can I be successful without one?" On the other hand, don't think that having a PhD is going to translate to success, because it's all mindset.

I dropped out of high school, got my GED, and joined the military at seventeen. And now, alongside my kids, Redline, my company, is my baby as well. I think for dad entrepreneurs out there, it is going to be difficult to have that work-life balance. There really isn't such a thing, especially when you are in the infant stages of growing a company. It definitely takes a lot of sacrifice. When you are starting a business, you have to look at it like a newborn baby. It needs constant attention, and it is going to be that way for a while. It will take a lot of attention on the weekends, nights, and you really get what you put into it.

Dating
and Social Life

HE WORLD MY kids are growing up in differs vastly from the one I grew up in. I guess parents of every generation could say the same thing. The major difference for kids growing up today is the technology. As a kid, I played outside until the streetlights came on, and if my mother needed us home earlier, she'd come find us. There was real freedom in that. We played football, basketball, and other games without adult supervision. We picked the teams, we made the rules, and we settled the arguments. We developed problem-solving skills that I feel have been robbed from this generation of kids.

In many ways, our society has tried to simulate natural childhood experiences with organized leagues for every sport, beginning at age four. Parents arrange "play dates" for kids to hang out with their friends. The smartphone allows us to track our kids at all times. And the smartphone has also enabled our kids to have access to unlimited information, both good and bad.

One of my biggest concerns as a father is the easy access to pornography. When I was a kid, if someone brought a *Playboy* magazine to school, he was the man! All the young men would huddle around him to sneak a peek at a naked woman, which is natural, healthy, male curiosity. Today, if a kid has a smartphone with internet access, a simple Google search of "naked woman" will flood their eyes with thousands of pictures and videos, many of which are extremely graphic.

Most of a modern teenager's social life takes place on social media. As I drive Uber on the weekends, I'm afforded a unique opportunity to observe the behavior of teenagers, to listen and learn from them as I prepare for my kids to hit the teenage social scene. My most disappointing observation is that many of these teenagers' communication skills are atrocious. Sometimes, even when they're riding in the same car, they communicate with each other through their phones. As quick as you can learn how to use Facebook and Instagram, they become outdated, and here come Snapchat and TikTok. I have little doubt that more are on the way.

As I write this, the oldest of my four children is in his first year of high school. He's about to hit all the major teenage experiences—driving, being introduced to drugs and alcohol, and, of course, dating. Now, I'd be lying if I said I wasn't more concerned with the thought of my daughter dating than my sons. My daughter is my youngest, and I pray that she'll have the opportunity to witness her brothers bring home girlfriends and observe how respectfully they treat them. I also pray that my boys will treat their girlfriends how they'd want their sister to be treated.

This all begins with me as their father and how they witness me treating my wife, their mother. One of the biggest benefits for me in creating *First Class Fatherhood* is that I've been able to ask seasoned dads how they handled the dating scene with their kids. In this chapter you'll read the responses from dads I've interviewed, when we discussed dating, social life, social media, and pornography. You'll even hear from a couple of dads with first-hand experience with child sex trafficking, who discuss how you can prevent your kids from falling victim.

Ken Daneyko

THREE-TIME NHL STANLEY CUP CHAMPION

WE KNOW THAT OUR KIDS need us when they are little children. They need you even more when they are young adults, believe it or not. That's what I've seen anyway. They need you as they start their lives and get into adulthood and out in the working world.

My son is still in college, and this is really when they need an ear to listen to them and understand them. I try to do that the best I can along the way. The dating thing was tough. My daughter is twenty-six, and I still treat her like she is fifteen years old. When she was in high school, I didn't pick her up much. I was always traveling with the New Jersey Devils, so her mother would pick her up most of the time. I only picked her up a handful of times. One time when she was fifteen and I picked her up, she was sitting on a picnic bench with about fifteen kids of which around seven or eight were guys.

Once I pulled up, all the guys scattered. All the girls came up to say hi to me. I've known most of them for a long time. When my daughter got in the car, I told her she could "introduce me to your guy friends, too, you know. It's okay, I won't bite." She goes, "Dad, are you kidding me? They are scared shitless of you! They've watched your fights on YouTube." I looked at her and said, "Good talk, sweetie. That's a good thing!"

I did kind of like that, but you want them to find the right person along the way who loves them and supports them. I feel grateful that I have a strong relationship with my kids and that I am able to be there now for them. When they were young, I was going through the ups and downs of my hockey career. I am grateful that I can be there a lot more for them now when they are adults and can have these conversations with them that, regretfully, I didn't have with them when they were younger.

Sean Duffy

FORMER UNITED STATES CONGRESSMAN, WISCONSIN

I THINK IT IS IMPORTANT for parents to educate their kids on issues they are going to confront, because if you don't do it as a parent, your school is going to do it or your culture is going to do it. Just because you don't talk to your kids about the issues doesn't mean someone else isn't. You want to engage them and have them think through some of these issues, and I think you'll be better off if you do it yourself as opposed to the school or the culture. Or have Hollywood do it for you or Google and Facebook do it for you.

Part of parenthood is bringing up issues that they face in the day that are cultural or political—to help them think through and form their own opinions. We have a lot of conversations about marijuana and the legalization of it. I'm opposed to it, and a lot of young people are in favor of it. So I have a lot of debates with my kids about it: What does it do to your motivation? What are the odds of you going from marijuana to a harder drug? What does it do to a young person's mind and how does it relate to psychosis?

So we will engage in that conversation. We talk about all the social issues. We don't always agree, but I am happy that my kids are thinking about it and asking questions about it. They sometimes come to different conclusions than I, but I am happy that they are being raised in a home where they are confronted with the issues and they are thinking about it and forming their own opinions, which I appreciate.

Mike Durant

NIGHTSTALKER PILOT, POW, BATTLE OF MOGADISHU

ONE OF OUR KIDS INVITED some friends to our lake house. There was alcohol involved, and we found out about it. We had the option to come down really hard on her or try to make a life lesson out of it. We chose to make a life lesson out of it.

We explained to her that it was wrong, and that she put us at risk. I pointed out to her that her having underage kids out here drinking alcohol, with the water here, creates a drowning risk. There is a driving risk. I asked her to think about all the things you put at risk for us when everything we do in our life is built around trying to help you be successful.

We told her we didn't want this to create a situation where we punish her for a period of time and that creates resentment. We wanted her to learn from her mistake. We told her that we were willing to forgive her, and we wanted her to tell us that she would never do this again.

I think that was one of the better decisions we ever made, because she appreciated the way that we handled it. She learned from her mistake; it never happened again, and she has turned into a fantastic young woman.

The risk you take if you come down a little too hard is your kids not talking to you and being honest with you. I'm not suggesting that you don't do anything about it at all, but it needs to be fair, and it needs to be measured. You need to find a balance between how hard you want to come down and still protect that relationship, because it is critical to have good communication throughout their lives and all the phases of friends and relationships. How you communicate with a four-year-old is dramatically different than when you are communicating with a seventeen-year-old or a twenty-year-old.

Scott Flansbaum

PARALYZED UNITED STATES MARINE

THE DATING STARTED WITH MY oldest girl. She came to us when she was in eighth grade and told us she wanted to date, and we said no. We joked and said not until you're thirty-five. But we know that is not realistic. We told her no and just explained to her why. We told her that she has so many things going on with school and sports and other stuff. We told her that we understood she wanted to experience having a boyfriend but that it was going to cause so much drama that she doesn't need in her life.

She was really upset and threw a temper tantrum. But about three days later, she went and talked to the boy and told him very respectfully that she was sorry and that she couldn't date him because her parents told her she couldn't. Guess what happened? The boy started trashing her at school, and three weeks later she came to us and told us that she hated this boy and was so glad that we told her not to date him. We told her to imagine if she had to go through all of that because she had started dating him. . . . We told her she didn't need that in her life at that time. Now that she is over sixteen, if she were to come and ask me again, which she hasn't, we would say yes.

We want our kids to have those experiences. Our youngest daughter went behind our backs when she was thirteen, and it created a lot of drama. She found out the hard way that we were right, and like every parent we said we don't tell you these things because we are geniuses, we tell you because we have lived through it. But I am excited now for my oldest daughter to come to us because she is ready.

I tell my girls that when you look at a lion pride, the female lion or lioness does all the work. She does the hunting, takes care of the kids, and does it all. The male lion sits there, and he's got that strong presence. So I tell them they can do everything and be as successful as you want—just look at your mom—but I want you guys to find a man that has a strong presence, that's gonna be there for you, that if you tell him you need him to get up and roar, he's going to do it for you and back you 100 percent.

Lee Goldberg

WABC-TV NEW YORK CHIEF METEOROLOGIST

WHEN IT CAME TIME FOR my kids to start dating, my daughter was first. Initially, when she was a little kid, she was more of a follower and an observer for a long time. As she got older, a strength sort of swelled through her, and I tapped into that. I reinforced it by telling her she was a strong young woman and that's how I wanted her to proceed in relationships. I told her in a relationship she doesn't have to let the other person drive things, to make sure she is comfortable with everything and to try and have balance.

I know you can go boyfriend, girlfriend crazy—I know I certainly did it with my wife growing up. My daughter is very balanced. So I just always tried to make sure she thought about herself, and not to identify as her and this boyfriend, but that it was her first and then let things develop from there. And you'll see even if in preschool a little boy comes up to your daughter, you'll be like, "Hey there, little guy, you have to deal with me first."

In terms of my son, my initial thought when he was growing up as a teenage boy was to make sure he was respectful. Treat girls the way you treat Mom.

Louis Gregory

FORMER UNITED STATES DEPARTMENT OF HOMELAND SECURITY DIRECTOR

THE WAY THAT THE WORLD is moving and the way that business is moving to a great extent involve social media, so I want my kids to have those skills. But I also want to monitor them. So I got on Twitter and Instagram, and I followed my kids.

I learned two things. One is they don't want you to follow them. Two, and this is really important for parents to know, these kids organize how they are going to prevent us as parents from knowing what they are doing, almost like counterintelligence. They create two Instagram accounts, and they call their fake Instagram account a finsta (fake Insta). You need to make it very clear to your kids that you want to know what their fake Instagram is. And do not take their word that they don't have one, because all of the kids I have interacted with, my daughter and her friends, they all do.

What's going on with your kids' social media is just as important as what's going on in their social life. I made it really clear that "I am the one who is paying your cell phone bill, and if you want to have that cell phone and want to use it, then I want to know what is going on." You have to set your expectations as a leader. As dads, we are leaders. In order to lead somebody, there are three ways to do it. You can lead by edict, you can lead by fear, or you can earn somebody's respect. And they are going to follow what you say because they believe in you; they know that you care for their best interests. That is the path that I tend to take. I want to let them know my expectations, and I also want them to know what will happen if they fail to meet those expectations.

Sean Hannity

HOST OF *HANNITY* ON FOX NEWS CHANNEL

I THOUGHT I WOULD BE worse than I am when my kids became old enough to start dating. When it comes to my daughter, I tell her, all boys ages thirteen through thirty, sorry, I don't believe any of them; they are full of crap. That's my line.

As far as my son, it is very simple. Treat women how you would want your own mother and your own sister to be treated. That's it. Everybody has feelings, and how you treat people matters. You don't want to hurt people. Be kind to people.

The number one rule I have for my kids is to never do drugs. Don't go near it. I understand with kids with weed that it is very popular; it's legal in some states, but I don't care. Don't touch that crap. To me it is a gateway drug. With my kids, that is a deal breaker with me.

I am not afraid of an eighteen-year-old kid drinking. I taught my kids about drinking. My line is don't be the dopey kid throwing up in the bushes. With drinking, people can run into some real serious problems. My kids knew of people who had problems with it, so they saw it. They saw the real agony and misery of addiction. I always made sure to point it out to them. I told my kids to never take a shot. Never drink a punch bowl. Stay away from hard liquor.

When it comes to drinking, everybody has a number. For some people, they have two drinks and they're out of it. I used to tend bar, and sometimes I've had people sit at the bar when I started my shift at 6:00 p.m., and at last call at 4:00 a.m. they are still there. You can still converse with them. They were functioning alcoholics. Some guys get all bravo and macho. Some girls get flirty if they go above their number. You have to know what your number is.

David Harris Jr.

CEO, UNCORKED HEALTH AND WELLNESS

I NEVER NOTICED IT, BUT my wife and daughters told me that whenever my girls would bring a boy to the house that I would always get more puffed up and talk with a deeper voice. I think tracking them and making sure they are where they are supposed to be is important. Your kid can be seemingly as innocent as possible, and you just never know where one little root started to grow inside their head that said they don't need to tell you everything and they can actually do something and get away with it.

We were fortunate that most of the time when our girls would do something like throw a party while we were away, we found out about it. So it would reinforce the fact that they shouldn't try to do stuff they thought they could get away with because we are going to find out about it anyway.

In hindsight I would say, make sure your kids are where they say they are going to be. Talk to the parents of your kids' friends. If they say they are going to someone's house, be sure you connect with the other person's parents and are on a talking basis with those parents. It is seemingly only getting worse what is going on in this world for our kids, and it takes a village to raise kids. I think that comes by making sure you are communicating with other parents of kids that are friends with your kids. Always make sure that you know where they are at, at all times. That is your job and role as a parent, so be forceful and make sure it is happening.

Merril Hoge

NFL VETERAN RUNNING BACK, FORMER ESPN ANALYST

I WAS IN THE GARAGE one day and my daughter starts telling me this joke. It was one I had heard before. As she was telling me the joke, I was thinking to myself, this is an X-rated joke that my daughter is telling me. When she told me the joke in the manner that she told me, an alarm went off. These are the kind of things she is hearing at school.

I thought to myself that I don't want some thirteen- or fourteen-year-old clueless kid giving my daughter some information when they are as clueless as she is. I realized then that they were starting to talk about sex and drugs, and I need to talk to her now about it.

I didn't want to create fear in my kids by telling them, "If you ever do anything like this, you're dead!" I wanted to help equip them with how to handle peer pressure. How to handle somebody who says, "You want a beer?" or "Do you want to smoke this joint?" I wanted to give them options and ways of getting out of those situations. We would walk through different scenarios, and I would tell them to make me the bad guy by saying, "If my dad finds out about this, we are all done!"

I would also tell my kids there are rewards in life for not using drugs and alcohol. I would tell them that I have never seen anybody in my lifetime who said that drugs and alcohol were the keys to their success. But I could give them thousands of stories about the lives it has ruined and opportunities it has ruined for people.

What I really tried to do was give them a full scope of things and ways to get out of peer pressure that they may be put into. Because of the relationship we developed, they knew they could always call me in a heartbeat. They knew they weren't going to get in trouble if they were in a bad environment. They were doing the right thing to get out of that environment, and I would be there to help them.

I gave them a lot of tools to use if someone tried to use peer pressure. I explained the fallout if they should choose to go down the wrong path. I would explain what happens if they have premarital sex and what could happen. Then I would say, "Here is what could happen if you say no." I would present both sides to them and provide them with tools. If kids never prepare for peer-pressure scenarios, they can get caught up in them. I've been in peer-pressure situations and collapsed in them because I didn't have an out. I didn't have a way to defend against it. So I have given my kids the tools to defend against it.

T. J. Houshmandzadeh

NFL VETERAN WIDE RECEIVER

THERE'S NOTHING THAT'S GOING to go on with my kids that I'm not aware of. I and my wife will always be there to help our kids navigate through a problem. We talk to them about real-life situations, especially with my daughter going off to college.

I'm going to talk to her about how boys are. My daughter is a beautiful young lady. So I tell her how I was in college, and things don't change. These boys are going to be the same way. I tell her what goes on in the locker room. This is what is talked about in the locker room. The knowledge that I give my daughter is like giving her the answers to a test beforehand, so she takes the test and doesn't fail it. That's what I do. I talk with my daughters.

I've been talking to my daughters about boys since they were twelve or thirteen years old. There is nothing that a boy can do that can "game" my daughter. You aren't going to sweet-talk my daughter. You aren't going to buy my daughter XYZ, because she's already had it. You are going to have to come with more than just the looks and the financial aspects of it.

They have been taught that from an early age. It's tough because eventually they are going to be on their own. They are going to be women. The boys will be men, and all you can do is try to impart the right things upon them. I teach my son to conduct himself with integrity. To make sure he is doing the right thing even when nobody is watching, because that is what being a good person is all about.

Hue Jackson

NFL HEAD COACH

AND FOUNDER OF STRANGER2CHANGER

HUMAN TRAFFICKING IS NOT AS well known as it should be. Anytime you have forty million victims, you would think that people would know more about this issue that has plagued America forever. This is a global industry for these particular people, where they are making between $90 billion and $120 billion a year.

Parents need to be educated on what human trafficking is and where it is happening. I think people would be amazed if they really just took a look. It might be in your community, it might be in your own backyard, and it may even be in your family. Parents need to be paying attention to this issue.

I think parents need to understand that these people who are preying on our children are very astute in all areas. They understand the social media platform world, and that is really where it starts. They have the ability to get victims through social media. My advice to every parent is to make sure you are involved with your kids on all social media and have access to their passwords. Pay attention to who they are communicating with online.

With a situation like the pandemic, kids are spending more time on the iPads, computers, and phones. Children can become victims of human trafficking just through social media. Parents may think they are doing the right thing by letting their kids have a phone or a device to spend time on, but you have to understand that these predators are finding ways into those devices to cause issues for your family.

Bob Kerrey

MEDAL OF HONOR RECIPIENT,

FORMER UNITED STATES SENATOR, NEBRASKA

IT'S DIFFERENT FOR MY SON and for my daughter when it comes to dating. With my son, I always told him to respect women and respect yourself. I know what it's like to have an amygdala that develops six or seven years before the prefrontal cortex does. You are going to get led around by desire. You're gonna want to know where that came from, and I'm not going to be there when you make the decision. So there are certain things you have to ask yourself, and they're your rules. The same thing is true with drugs and other things that can get you in trouble. I won't be there with you when it comes time to make that decision with women.

Now with my daughter, as soon as she goes through puberty, she can get pregnant, and there is no going back from that moment. If you're pregnant, you're pregnant, and now you have three choices and all of them are really hard choices to make. If you decide to carry the baby, you're a parent and you are a parent forever. It's a good thing, not a bad thing, but it is a real thing.

In my case, I would tell my kids they have a special status: you're the son or daughter of a governor or senator, so do not bitch to me if you are at a party and people are drinking underage and you get busted and the headline says, "Governor Kerrey's Daughter Gets Arrested!" You get lots of things that are good being the child of a member of the Senate or governor, so don't bitch if you get something bad as a consequence of that status. With status comes responsibility. Both good and bad.

Travis Lively

NAVY SEAL VETERAN, SCREENWRITER

I WAS IN MY ROOM shaving one night, and my daughter came in with my wife. My daughter says, "Dad, I'm gay." I looked at her and said, "Yeah, I know," and just kept shaving. My wife and I have always known.

I am still figuring this out. This is a different dynamic that I didn't grow up with. It is something that we are still working our way through. She has a lot of girlfriends, but I don't know which one she's dating or which one she's not. They are all great kids that hang out together. My daughter has always shown me that she can be trusted to do the right thing, so I just roll with the punches and see where this is going to go. I only know what I don't know at this point.

My wife and daughter are extremely close. They are super tight, like *Gilmore Girls* tight. So I am usually finding things out when they are five days old and things are already settled down. My wife thinks I can process it that way better. I don't think they give me enough credit, because I am pretty socially liberal. But at the same time, as long as my daughter has that candor with my wife and they have that kind of relationship, then I still win. I'm here on standby to always keep my promises and make sure she doesn't disrespect her mom and let her know that I have her back no matter what happens.

Pat McNamara

RETIRED DELTA FORCE OPERATOR
AND FOUNDER OF TMACS INC

ONE THING THAT I AM contending with is gender confusion nowadays. It's a real thing. When we were growing up, if there was a gay guy in the class it was because he was gay. He didn't choose that, that's just the way he is, that's just the way he was wired.

Nowadays you get to pick your gender. You get to actually pick it. It's crazy, so that's one of the things that I struggle with my daughter about because she identifies one way and I'm all good with it.

My kids and I have a really good, open, honest relationship. There are no secrets, I don't patronize them, and I'm never condescending. We have a really good, trusting bond. They allow me to follow all of their social media, and sometimes I learn more about them on social media than from talking to them, because that's where they live. It drives me crazy. Because of all this technology, communication skills are dying and that can be a struggle.

I make sure that I drive conversations with them and lead by example. Whenever I am out with them, I am never on my phone. I drive the conversation so we can have an intellectual discourse. I give them sound, honest advice, I mean brutally honest advice, and they love it. They appreciate that and respect that.

One of the things right now with kids is that they are being cyberbullied. My daughter is very sensitive to that. So I show her some of the comments people throw at me. I have a massive following on the internet. I show her some of the nasty comments where people just bash me on there and tell her that it doesn't bother me. I mean people give me a pretty good bashing, but I could care less.

Chris Osman

UNITED STATES MARINE AND NAVY SEAL VETERAN

WHEN MY DAUGHTER BECAME old enough to start dating, I talked to the dads. I didn't mess with the boys because that's my daughter, and I trust my daughter. So if she is making a choice and she thinks a guy is cute, then great, who am I to say that he's not. I look back at pictures of myself, and I was a skinny dork. My nose was too big for my face, and I was just a little punk. I can only imagine what the dads of the girls I was chasing thought about me.

So I always talk to the dads, not now that she is an adult but when she was a teenager. I would have conversations with the dads and say that I understand, and I get it that your son is young. I was his age, you were his age, and think back to what we were after at that age. So here's the deal: kids are kids and they're gonna do what they're gonna do. I don't believe any kid is a saint, and kids do stuff that their parents never find out about, just like there were things I did that my parents never found out about.

But I'm not going to lie and say I am not concerned about her health and her safety and her well-being. Your son is a minor and you are an adult. So let them date and let them do their thing, but if he beats her, if he tries any shenanigans, I am coming back to your house and beating your ass. I would tell them that I can't do anything to their son, but you are in charge of your son and how he acts and treats women. So that is a direct reflection on you, and I will hold you personally responsible. I get it that kids are kids, and they will date, laugh, cry, and break up. That's no big deal, that's just kid stuff. I'm talking about the real serious stuff. Any of that, and I'm coming back to the dad's house.

I've had that conversation with a couple of dads, and I've never had a problem. I think you have to be real with people, and if the dad takes it the wrong way, then he takes it the wrong way. I'm not in charge of his feelings.

As far as dating when it came to my son, he is gay, and my whole mentality with him dating is the same way.

Bubba Page

ENTREPRENEUR AND INVESTOR

WE HAVE BEEN TEACHING our kids even as young as five and six years old about the harms of pornography. It's not like we are showing it to our kids and saying don't look at this. We are teaching our kids that their bodies are sacred. Their bodies are private. And we teach them about inappropriate touching. We tell them that nobody should be touching them. Nobody should be looking at you there, and you shouldn't be looking at anybody whether that's in person or on a screen. Those are things that will have a negative impact on their lives.

We keep all of our computers and devices out in the open. Nothing is hidden, and we don't have TVs or computers in individual rooms. We have a family computer that is out in the open in the family room. One time my wife was helping my son, who was seven at the time, and he typed in "dirt bike clip art" for a school project. Several images down was the backside of a nude woman sitting on a dirt bike, and my son yelled out "Pornography!" My wife came running over to X out of the screen. He did that because we taught him what pornography is, and we are training our kids that it is not appropriate. That happened in our own home with all the filters and everything on our computer.

Dads need to talk with their kids about the dangers of pornography and the painful effects it can have on their lives. It can have a negative effect on their real-life relationships. It can affect the expectations of intimacy in marriage. It will only take away and it will never give. It seems like, growing up, pornography was totally fine, that it was okay, so why not? It didn't hurt anybody. You're just looking at it, but the reality is, more studies are coming out saying that more people are getting addicted to pornography. It is causing major problems with people's ability to have real relationships.

I would suggest for dads out there to check out Fight the New Drug. They have a ton of good resources for anybody struggling with porn addiction. If you are a dad who is bringing that filth into your home, once you remove it, it will free you from a weight that you may not even know is on your shoulders and help you become a better father and a better husband.

Kelly Pavlik

FORMER BOXING WBO, WBC,
LINEAL MIDDLEWEIGHT CHAMPION

I AM TOTALLY AGAINST BULLIES. I don't like it, and it's one big thing that I am really against. I tell my kids to be nice and respectful to everybody. I tell them to treat everyone the way they want to be treated. But if somebody tries to put harm on you or gets in your face, I tell them to do what they gotta do.

The first punch could be the last punch and can cause serious injury, so I tell them to do what they have to do to protect themselves and not let people walk on them. My daughter has run into a bullying problem, and I told her to avoid the girl. She told me that she couldn't, and then I told her to go and talk to the teachers. So she did that and we finally got it worked out. But it came to a point where I told her that if this girl gets in your personal space and you feel threatened, I said maybe you're just going to have to take care of it. And we worked on that part of it, but thank God it never came to that.

I do not want my kids being cocky or being bullies or starting any trouble. I just want them to go about their business and have fun with their friends, and if they get bullied or they see bullying going on, we always tell them to stick up for the one getting bullied. The old saying goes that the only way to beat a bully is to stand up to them. And I have found that to be true. If you stand up to a bully and even if you get beat up but you put a good fight up, the bully isn't going to bother you anymore.

Mike Pompeo

FORMER UNITED STATES SECRETARY OF STATE

WHEN OUR SON BECAME old enough to start dating, my wife and I tried to coach him to make good decisions. We put some limitations on it too. The places he could go, how often, and how frequently. We made sure that we were part of that to the extent that we could be. We also reminded him that this was a transition and that he had an obligation to treat everyone he encountered, including the young women that he was dating, to treat them with dignity and respect and to treat them appropriately as well. Those messages, I think, resonated very much with Nick. And then we reminded him, too, to cherish every minute as you mature and as you grow up and as you look for that person that you will partner with in your life, to make sure that you're doing it in the right way and you're finding a set of shared values with which you can build your family unit.

Michael Rutledge

NIGHTSTALKER PILOT AND NAVY SEAL VETERAN

IT'S INEVITABLE. YOU CAN'T DENY the whole sexuality thing. I think the worst thing a parent can do is lock them down and pretend that it doesn't exist, because it certainly does.

We tried to deal with it very early on in a healthy manner. Even when they were ten, eleven, or twelve, when they start getting curious, we told them it was healthy. We tried to explain to them that what they were feeling was healthy and normal. We went through the whole sex talk and all that kind of stuff and tried to keep it out of the shadows.

Since we have sons, what we told them that seemed to have the biggest impact as far as the physical aspect and dating was, one, when you are dating, you're not just dating to have fun; in reality, you are looking for the person you are going to marry. So if you don't think you are going to marry her, don't make it physical. It's okay to get to know people and have fun and find out what you like and don't like. Just remember the whole purpose of dating is to find out who you are going to marry.

Two, when you decide what kind of physical relationship you are going to have with this girl, just remember, when you get married to your wife, how many guys do want her to have had her lips on? So we try to put it in that perspective.

As far as taking responsibility as young men, our final lesson to them was that we understand hormones and passion and all that kind of stuff, because we were sixteen, seventeen, and eighteen. She may not appreciate it now, but if you say no and you take care of her and honor her—she may not appreciate it at sixteen or seventeen, but I guarantee when she is twenty-five or twenty-six and gets ready to get married, she may not even re-member your name, but she will remember the one guy who said, "Hey, let's not. You're a sweet girl. Let me cherish you and send you on your way." I know that sounds really outdated and old-fashioned, but that is what our thought process was on the whole dating scene.

Craig Sawyer

NAVY SEAL VETERAN,

FOUNDER OF VETS FOR CHILD RESCUE (V4CR)

OUR DAUGHTER WAS ABDUCTED in Tucson, Arizona, from a Subway sandwich parking lot by a local lifetime criminal at knifepoint. He took her and brutally assaulted her for hours. I got a call from my daughter in the middle of the night, and as you can imagine, it was a very upsetting phone call to get. Her attacker was apprehended, and months after her attack, we officially founded and got 501(c)(3) status for Veterans for Child Rescue.

Child sex trafficking is the fastest growing criminal enterprise on Earth. In short order it will be larger than the narcotics traffick-ing trade. Parents need to watch after their kids and know what is going on with their phones and with their friends and with their online use, because a lot of these predators, instead of just being creepers hanging around on the playground and shopping malls, now they are stalking your children online. We may think that we lock our windows and our doors at night and our children are safe in their bedrooms, but they are not safe at all because the child that they think they are interacting with on their cell phone, their com-puter, or even their Xbox game could very well be a predatory adult that is deceiving your kid and working them into a compromised position.

We as parents have to assert ourselves and get in there and find out who our children are dealing with and what apps they are using. Some of these apps not only have audio and video recording capabilities, but they have geolocating on it. The child might not even know that the predator can tell not only what state, city, and neighborhood they are in but even which bedroom in the house they are in. And the poor child has no idea, and the predator can be sitting in a car out front waiting for the kid to take out the garbage, and they could be snatched up and you never see them again.

We have to pay attention to their phones. That's the new killing fields. That's how they are gaining access and stalking our children.

Jim Shockey

OUTFITTER, AUTHOR, HOST OF *JIM SHOCKEY'S THE PROFESSIONALS* AND *UNCHARTED*

WHEN THEY BECAME OLD ENOUGH to start dating, it was definitely different with my daughter and my son. My wife made it abundantly clear to me to keep my nose out of it when it came to my daughter.

My side of the house, the man-cave side of the house, is filled with mounted animals, skeletons, and crazy stuff. It was difficult for my daughter to find a boyfriend with me as a father, because word would get around and her friends would tell the tale of walking into my crypt filled with all kinds of unusual things that I've gathered from around the world. It wasn't easy for her. She would have to find somebody really dumb or really confident. And thank

God she had a lot of her mother in her. She had good common sense, and hopefully I helped with that along the way.

But I was told in no uncertain terms to keep my nose out of her business and not threaten any of these young boys that were chasing her around. It was difficult as a father to stand by, especially when you know that so many of them aren't worth spending five minutes with, let alone months and months or a lifetime.

Our son is pretty private about all that, and I didn't know much about any girl he may have been dating until he introduced us to the young lady that he married.

Out of the three and a half billion guys out there and the three and a half billon women out there, I couldn't have personally chosen better spouses for both of my kids. So it's probably best that I kept my nose out of it. If you raise your children right, you don't have to worry about that. They are going to make the right choices because they have pride in who they are, and they don't want to spend the rest of their lives with someone who treats them any less. So it all starts with child-rearing.

Jeff Timmons

SINGER, SONGWRITER, 98 DEGREES

WHEN MY OLDEST BECAME ELIGIBLE to hit the dating scene—and alcohol, drugs, and all of that was introduced—I lived in Las Vegas. So you can imagine what was surrounding my kids. It's a very transient town; it's a party town, and although there are other parts of Vegas besides the Strip, all of those trappings are right there and in full effect. My oldest didn't really go through a whole lot of that. I'm sure she experimented with some things.

I'm a liberal guy. I'm in the entertainment business and I'm an artist, so I have been around it all and seen it all. Part of that environment still exists when you do after-parties; I was out late sometimes after we performed gigs to make appearances, and I was always around all that stuff. So it was hard for me to say "Don't do this!" when I am surrounded by it, although they know I didn't participate in all that stuff.

It was a tough experience for me, but I experienced a lot of that stuff later, after they left the house, that rebellious stage. Because of our life circumstance—our family dynamic is so extraordinarily different than most people—I think I am experiencing a lot of this stuff with my oldest kids now. Not in a crazy rebellious way, but now they are off into college and that environment. But I had an easy time with my three oldest kids, and I didn't have much friction with them. But I have two more to go.

Andre Tippett

NFL HALL OF FAME LINEBACKER

THE THING I REALLY IMPRESSED upon my kids when it came to dealing with friends or when they were hanging out in social situations was to do for others who can't do for themselves. Protect those who can't protect themselves.

Growing up, I was oldest in my family, and I was always big for my age. I was constantly being challenged. And it wasn't the fact that I was afraid to confront people, but it was never a fair fight. It was always some guy that had three or four of his buddies hanging around, and he wanted to confront me because I was the big kid in the class. I always knew it was never going to end in a fair fight, so

I was constantly ducking and running and avoiding a ton of guys that were freaking bullies that, to this day, I look to run into just to have a conversation with them.

So, especially with my girls, I was big on telling them to protect those that can't protect themselves. And if you see somebody who is being bullied or someone who is being taken advantage of, step in and help them. All three of my kids are like that.

Allen West

FORMER CONGRESSMAN, ARMY LIEUTENANT COLONEL

MY DAUGHTERS SEE HOW I RESPECT and treat my wife, that I am not intimidated by the fact that she has an MBA and a PhD. She is a brilliant woman and a financial advisor and a broker. We complement each other. That is how you set up future relationships for your children, because they will go out and look to replicate that positive aspect they have seen in their own lives.

One thing my mother taught me was that a man must stand for something or else he will fall for anything, and we need to get back to those basic fundamentals of fatherhood. We need to talk about what it means to be a responsible man in the home. As we lose that, we are going to lose the essence of what our country is. This is not to say that a woman alone cannot raise kids and be successful at it, but I think that when you have both strong male and strong female role models, and when you have a man that says, "This is how you treat a woman"—that's what my daughters see.

As parents you have to live your life by example. You can't say these are the things you shouldn't do and then you go out and do something totally different. That is the hypocrisy of being a parent and the hypocrisy of leadership. Proverbs 22:6 says, "Train up a child in the way that they should go so that when they grow old they shall not depart from it." It's those everyday little lessons that you have to impart to them, and they will remember and think about them.

Heck, just a few days ago, I thought about some things my dad used to say to me.

Rod Woodson

NFL HALL OF FAME DEFENSIVE BACK, SUPER BOWL CHAMPION

WELL, I TOLD MY GIRLS to never believe boys. Just don't believe them, because boys lie. I know who I was as a kid, and I think about all the other boys out there who are very similar. I wasn't the nicest father to the boys who came to my house, I can be honest about that. I would not talk to them a whole bunch and always tried to keep them guessing as to whether I liked them or not.

But my girls are very strong girls, like alpha girls, and they don't take too much sarcasm or anything like that from boys. They are willing to speak their minds and be honest with who they are, and I think they know their worth. That is the hardest thing. I think the hardest thing with girls is to teach them to understand the value of who they are, that they don't have to settle for a certain type of person. They can look for the best type of person, someone who is going to treat them like a human being, the way they should be treated. That's the main thing growing up as a father of three girls.

My oldest was kind of refreshing because she is really an alpha girl. She's a chef who works in Las Vegas in one of Caesars's steak restaurants, and I think my younger girls followed suit with her because they saw how strong she was; so that was refreshing. My wife is the opposite; she is more of a nurturer and a giver. My girls kind of took after me with the stubbornness and being very transparent with people at times, which sometimes is not the best thing to do. They learned that they are special, and they are only going to be around men who treat them as such.

Faith, Values, and Service

I'LL BELIEVE IT *when I see it.* For most of my life, that was my philosophy. I'm the son of a used car salesman from the Bronx, New York. I grew up idolizing a fast-paced hustler mentality that led me to believe that the only way to get ahead in life was to get over on people.

Because of this poor philosophy, I've traveled down some dark roads in my life. But when I made a commitment to myself to make positive changes in my life, I was led to a path of personal development. I started reading books by Napoleon Hill, James Allen, Jim Rohn, Wayne Dyer, and also read the Bible. During this journey, I discovered that having faith was the complete opposite of my limited belief of "I'll believe it when I see it."

To truly live by faith means that once you believe it, then you'll see it. The Bible describes faith in Hebrews 11:1 as the assurance of things hoped for, the conviction of things not seen. As I began to change the way I was thinking, everything else in my life began to change. It has improved all facets of my life, from my relationship with my wife to launching my podcast, *First Class Fatherhood.*

The thing is, once I began to see results materialize as a result of my belief in them coming to pass, it drove me further and further away from my old philosophy, which at one point resulted in a lifetime ban from Giants Stadium. However, my new philosophy resulted in the NFL inviting me to be on the field for two Super Bowl media days, during which I've had the opportunity to interview players and coaches such as Tom Brady, Richard Sherman, Bill Belichick, and Andy Reid.

Hundreds of podcasters have reached out to me asking me how I've been able to land such incredible guests for my show. I answer them in the same way. "Read Mark 11:24," which states, "Whatsoever you ask for in prayer, believe that you have received it, and it will be yours." Most of the time, I get a smart remark or an eye-roll emoji in return.

For those who are willing to listen, I add one other verse, 1 John 5:14-15, which states: "This is the confidence we have in approaching God: that if we ask anything according to His will, He hears us. And if we know that He hears us in whatever we ask, we know that we already have what we have asked of Him." It's not a matter of believing you're gonna get it—it's knowing that you already have it.

This concept is similar to ordering something from Amazon. Most people order from Amazon and then expect the package to arrive. They have faith that Amazon will deliver. I have found that God is even more reliable than Amazon. This may sound suspicious to some who read this, but as someone who has stood in the presence of the president of the United States at the White House with press credentials—me, a railroad mechanic with no journalism experience, among all the White House correspondents—I can assure you that faith works.

Unfortunately, several dads I've interviewed have had to bury one of their children, and I asked them how that experience has affected their faith. Of course, not all dads are men of faith, and I don't claim that my way of thinking is any better than anyone else's—only that it's better than the way I once thought. As Friedrich Nietzsche said, "You have your way. I have my way. As for the right way, the correct way, and the only way, it does not exist."

Over the years, I also discovered that getting over on people doesn't lead to sustained happiness. Serving other people does. I've had the honor of speaking with those who have dedicated much of their lives to serving others. I often ask the dads on *First Class Fatherhood* what top values they hope to instill in their kids as they grow up, and the idea of service is frequently part of their response.

In the pages that follow, you'll read responses from dads I've interviewed on *First Class Fatherhood* as we spoke about faith, service, and values.

Glenn Banton

CEO OF OPERATION SUPPLY DROP

IT'S A WONDERFUL EXPERIENCE TO volunteer with your kids. There are many ways you can volunteer as a family to help our nation's veteran community. Some of the easiest ways to do that is to see if there is a veteran's home somewhere nearby, or a VFW hall, and reach out.

A lot of it is just getting your kids around that type of experience. We think of veterans as kind of the older generation, yet there are many young veterans now. But I think one of the most interesting ways we can introduce kids to that world is by hearing some of the older veterans. There is a level of wisdom that is shared by not just their service but also just the time in their life. To be able to dig in and hear those stories . . . You can reach out to your local city or local town and find out what type of veteran organizations exist.

Something that we really focus on at OSD is the family units. Even as we continued to grow and evolve over the years, the main thing and main word on the top of our whiteboard was *family*. A lot of the challenges in the military trickle back into the family—is the family happy? I think what a lot of the general public fails to realize is the spouse and kids at home, their happiness and their ability to find fulfillment, is one of the biggest factors in allowing a service member to stay in. It would be nice for the service members with ten or more years who have acquired a lot of wisdom to be able to stay in the military to pass it on to the next generation.

My kids are heavily involved with volunteering and helping out the veteran community. My daughter volunteers in our warehouse, and she helps with content creation. My son loves to join the events. Some of his favorite people are my friends who are amputees. He got involved with this back when he was six or seven, and he was meeting these veterans with bionic limbs, and he thought they were so cool.

I really love to have my kids around this type of service for them to get a chance to see and understand that all of these veterans and their families and their situations are all different, and so we need to get to know each of them.

Jack Brewer

NFL VETERAN SAFETY

THE FAMILY IS GOD. God is the Father, the Father in the spirit, we need a father in the flesh, but it is very difficult to get that father in the flesh when you haven't established the importance of the Father in the spirit.

As dads, we need to be that spiritual balance for our children. We need to be the vehicle that shows and represents Christ to our kids. That's really difficult when you have a society where your public schools, your government agencies, and more are outcasting faith-based organizations and faith by not allowing prayer in every part of our society, not allowing our government funding to go to organizations that are faith based. Those things must stop, and it has to come to an end.

When you look at the fatherless crisis in our nation, we really have to be committed to get into the root. Too many things are going against the patriarch and going against fatherhood, taking down and watering down masculinity, which has been happening across the nation. Through Christ our bodies are the same as our wives, and we need each other. We can't get to the point where we are motivating people in promoting the breakup of the home and women without men. That is not leading, and that is really causing a lot of the ills that we see in society. The stats themselves speak for themselves.

I pray that my kids find their truth through the Word of God. I think that is the foundation of any man or woman. That's where you get your truth. I think that if you really home in to the Word of God and study the Word of God, I think you will be able to make clear decisions. I think your morality will stay intact, and then I think you can really be a member of society who is there for the good, who shows true love.

Tim Brown

NFL HALL OF FAME WIDE RECEIVER

IN THE BEGINNING OF MY Hall of Fame speech, I mentioned that I wake my kids up every day and say to them that this is a day the Lord has made, and we shall rejoice and be glad in it.

My kids didn't get a chance to see most of my football career. My son said something to me when I found out that I was going to be in the NFL Hall of Fame. I immediately called somebody to share the good news, and my son was sitting next to me, and he heard me say, "Yeah, this probably should have happened a few years earlier." My son, who was twelve years old at the time, waited until I got off the phone and he said to me, "Hey, Dad, think about this. If this would have happened six years ago and you went in as a first-ballot Hall of Famer, my sister and I would not have understood it. Now we do. We get it today."

And I was like, oh man, I feel like such a heel. He really helped put things in perspective, and that experience meant so much to them and me. God knows my heart, and I do many speaking engagements and a lot of charity work. I am part of the team of youth leaders at our church, so I am totally active in the community. I am trying to do as much as I can possibly do to make sure that the big guy in the sky is happy with what's happening down here.

Raising kids in that manner is not the easiest thing to do because sometimes you are not the coolest dad around. You're not going to go out on the dance floor and shake your butt around and drink alcohol and do all this other stuff. Sometimes your kids don't understand that. I know they will one day. My oldest does. He gets it because he saw a little bit of me before I became fully committed. So, from that standpoint, it is an incredible life, and I wouldn't give it up for anything in the world. The trials and tribulations may be what they are, but we know at the end we are going to be victorious; so that is the name of the game.

Nick Carter

SINGER, ACTOR, MUSICIAN, BACKSTREET BOYS

THE HARDEST PART ABOUT WANTING to help people during the COVID-19 pandemic was having to be responsible by staying at home and following the guidelines. You see all of these things happening through social media and how the pandemic was actually affecting people's lives and, of course, the frontline responders and all of the essential workers out there who were working endlessly and tirelessly every single day. The nurses and doctors that were risking their lives to save the lives of other people.

As I was watching this on TV, I wanted to jump in my car and drive to the hospital and deliver water or food or do whatever I could to help. I teamed up with Voss, and we had this idea of delivering thousands of bottles of water to the Mount Sinai Hospital. New York City was heavily affected by the pandemic, as were other places all throughout the country. We were able to do that, and all of the doctors and nurses received the water, and they were really grateful for it.

It feels good to give back in any way that we can. When the pandemic first struck, we did something with Fox. We did a benefit with Elton John, and we have been trying to find creative ways to give back while we had to be responsible and stay at home. I know that my children are watching me, and the kind of father that I want to be is a loving, inspirational, and educating father.

Ryan Clark

NFL VETERAN SAFETY, SUPER BOWL CHAMPION

OUR KIDS ARE ABSOLUTELY INVOLVED in our community. We have chosen schools for them where community service is part of the curriculum. They go to schools where you have to have a certain amount of community service hours in order to move on to the next grade and in order to graduate. I think that is awesome.

We also, as a family, being that we are blessed with a lot of things, have an opportunity to help other people. We make sure that we are giving. We make sure that not only are we visible from the efforts that we do with our time, but also monetarily. I think that is something that our kids need to understand: to whom much is given, much is required.

I think it is cool to be a part of a family that is one with a heart of compassion and one with a heart of empathy. My wife is involved in various things, and that helps me be more involved because sometimes you can get so busy that you don't focus on some of the little things that you can do with your time. So it has really been awesome to make service to the community a family effort.

Brian Deegan

MOST DECORATED MOTOCROSS DRIVER
IN X GAMES HISTORY

I FEEL LIKE FAITH IS the foundation of everything in our house. Could we be more hard-core about it, yes. I get up and pray every morning and every night before I go to bed. It helps me start my day. We pray at the dinner table every night as a family. Those are things that were just normal back in the day. Now I think everyone gets so busy and everybody has something to do, so they're like, "Oh, I gotta go," and everyone goes their own separate ways.

I think that there are simple basics in raising a family the right way and keeping things solid, and I believe that way is having faith as a foundation—having a foundation in faith, church, and community and doing things together.

I am fortunate that, because of racing, our family gets to spend a lot of time together. My job is to be with my kids, promote their sponsors and endorsement deals, and their racing careers. Eating dinner together or at least eating one meal a day as a family is important. One thing I've noticed is that some families will go around the dinner table and each person will say one good thing that happened during the day. Having any kind of conversation instead of just heads down looking at the phone.

Spending time is important, and so is faith. It took me until almost dying in a crash. I had a really bad crash doing an MTV show, where I did a back flip and came up short, and the handlebar went through my stomach. I blew out my kidney and my spleen and almost bled to death. By the time I got to the hospital, I was bleeding out and passing in and out.

That's when I started praying and saying, please, God, if You are real, I don't want to die. I was thinking about my daughter; I was thinking about my funeral. The doctor leaned over me and asked me if there was anything I'd like to say to my family, so I thought I was gonna die. On the way into emergency surgery, that's when I really started praying and that's when I gave my life to Christ.

I woke up with tubes everywhere, my wife was sick in the hospital, and we found out she was pregnant with our son. As all of these events were unfolding, I thought it was too much of a coincidence and thought I have to go this route. Once I did that, I fully focused on being a Christian.

I think a lot of people are lost without faith right now. I hate that they are pushing it out of everything. I hate that they are making Christians or even God-fearing people weirdos, as if you're weird for being into God. I hate that. If you don't believe the Bible, I'm okay with that as long as you have read the Bible. If you haven't read the Bible, then don't tell me you're not into it. It took me reading the New Testament for God to really speak to me, and at that point I couldn't turn back from it. Without faith, I would be a mess.

Derick Dillard

REALITY TV STAR, *COUNTING ON*

MY DAD PASSED AWAY WHILE I was in college, and I began thinking about how short life really is and what really matters and what doesn't matter so much that people put a lot of weight on.

I was a part of a church at that time in college, and missions were very important. Going and helping people who are less fortunate and sharing the hope of the gospel. I had never done that personally. I was very supportive of it but never had a calling for it.

With that focused realization that life is short and brief, I made a commitment to go to Nepal for two years. I know a lot of kids go backpacking in Europe after college. I really wanted to have a focused direction at that time and give back to others. My philosophy was to make the most of each opportunity in life, whether that's as a single person, a father, or a married man without children.

Wherever you are in your path in life, there's never an end of life until you die. It's not like life ends when you become a dad, although many people portray it that way, as if when you have kids all of your fun things are in your past. I try to make the most out of whatever stage of life I'm in, so I've learned a lot about that from people who have taught me along the way.

When I got back from Nepal, I got married to a wonderful woman, we had a child, and we took a position with a mission organization in Central America. We worked down there for two years trying to help gang communities gain life skills and job skills, to have an honest way of making a living instead of the gang lifestyle. Things have changed a lot—now I'm currently in law school—but everything is an adventure, and I wouldn't change any of it for the world.

Gunnar Hanson

NAVY SEAL VETERAN, PASTOR

I WAS NOT A RELIGIOUS person at all growing up. I made it through Navy SEAL training, and shortly after checking into SEAL Team 3, I went out and got drunk and went out driving. I got arrested for resisting and evading arrest at twenty years old. Over the course of the next eighteen months, I lost my security clearance and ultimately got it back.

But during that window, my life kind of fell apart. I had a friend who was a Christian who nagged me to go to church, and I finally conceded. I went once, and through that time I accepted Christ as my savior and then began the journey of trying to figure out how did being a Navy SEAL and being a Christian fit together.

Ultimately, my master's thesis was on "The Christian in Combat." One of my passions became helping people who carry arms to protect people how to reconcile the use of force and their faith. One of the cruxes is the commandment "Thou shall not murder," which many people confuse by saying "Thou shall not kill." It's actually "Thou shall not murder." Murder and killing are two different words from the Hebrew text.

There is a difference between murdering somebody and justifiable self-defense or taking another human life in a different circumstance. There is a misconception, and the argument carries over to Romans 13 that talks about how God has established the authority to protect society from evildoers and it doesn't bare the sword in vain. So the heart of it is, anybody who serves, law enforcement or military, when they are doing it, they are not representing themselves; they stand for the authorities that are over them, and so they function in the capacity of administering justice for the government.

In most cases, especially law enforcement, use of force is for the protection of their own life or protection of another's life. In the military, it gets a little more complicated, but within the context of the United States, every soldier, if they don't function according to the Judeo-Christian ethics that our country was founded on, they will be held accountable. There's plenty of law enforcement and military members in jail for not using force in accordance with law.

Mike Haynes

NFL HALL OF FAMER

WHEN I WAS FIRST DIAGNOSED with prostate cancer, I didn't want anyone to know. I didn't want people to feel sorry for me. I told my wife, let's just keep it between us. For some reason I just thought that my life was going to come to an end, and I had never seen this coming. The doctors were telling me that I was fortunate because we caught it in the early stages when it's treatable and that I was going to be fine. Even though they were telling me that, I thought they were just being nice.

The moment I started talking about it, everything started to change. I told a total stranger about it when I was on an airplane. Like I normally do when I go on a plane, I'll ask the person next to me if they are going home or where are you heading. This woman said she was going to New York and that she was meeting her friend there to go on vacation. Then she asked me where I was going, and I told her that I had just been diagnosed with prostate cancer. She said, "Oh, I'm an oncology nurse!" So we started talking and she made me feel totally comfortable that we did find out in the early stages and that I am going to be fine.

That opened the door for me to talk about it more and I shared it with my mom and my boss at the NFL. The more I shared it, the better I felt about it. I realized this was going to be important for me going forward. I got through it, and later I was asked to be the spokesperson for prostate cancer. I thought that was an excellent opportunity to serve and give back, and so I did it gladly.

Jim Kelly

NFL HALL OF FAME QUARTERBACK

IN THE BEGINNING WHEN MY SON was diagnosed with a fatal disease, I was one of those guys who went the total opposite. My wife sought the Lord and I ran. I was mad, I was frustrated, and I asked why He would put me through all these things in my life. From losing four Super Bowls in a row, not just over my career but in a row, and then You give me a son who was born with a fatal genetic disease?

I was mad and my wife was the complete opposite. She went to seek the Lord and I ran. It took me a little while to understand why I needed God in my life, and then after a while I got it. I wish I would've done it sooner, but the old phrase is "It's God's perfect timing." It taught me who I am; living through my son. He taught me toughness, really, the way I saw him live, and the bottom line is that I needed to change my life.

I was not a really good husband, and this is all part of the upcoming movie about my life, and it is also covered in my wife's book, which is a *New York Times* bestseller. Those were things that you learn over time, and I did through all of this. I realized I needed to change my life, and I did. I am so much better off now because of it.

Then, of course, I was hit with cancer three times, and I could've easily just said, "God, why?" I had already gone through all of that, and I know the reason I am still here now and all of the things I went through, I understand why God put me through all of that. It was to put me where I am at today, and that is being able to make a difference for others out there. Whether they are battling cancer as a kid or as an adult, whether they are not having a good life and their marriage is not going the way they want it to, or if there's young kids who want to give up on life—there are so many things I understand why I had to go through all of this, but I get it now. I thank God for it.

Andrew Klavan

EDGAR AWARD–WINNING AUTHOR

I THINK THE FATHERLESS CRISIS is a tremendous crisis, but I think it is part of a larger crisis. I believe the fatherless crisis is one of the worst symptoms of a disease that has infected the modern mind: let's call it the disease of materialism. The idea that all we are, are these meat puppets with chemistry sets inside and that we have no spiritual values. That there is no moral world in which we can discover through wisdom and through exploration and through thinking and through life experience. That we are just these pieces of meat floating around from the cradle to the grave.

If you think about that, if you think about how children cost you money, it's not like the old days where they take over the farm or take over your business. They are largely an economic outlay. The only things you are receiving from them are spiritual benefits. You have the spiritual benefit of bringing new spirits into the world, and you are helping shape those spirits as they were meant to be.

But if you don't look at the world like that, if you just look at the world as a series of pleasures and pains, if you just look at the world as the greatest thing you can do is succeed in your career, be comfortable, have a lot of money, have a lot of sex, then why would you have kids? Why would you commit yourself to one woman, why would you commit yourself to a marriage that might have difficulties you have to navigate through? The underlying ethos of materialism—that there is nothing else there but our material comfort, our material goods, our wealth, our comfort, and that's all there is to life—has been very, very destructive.

I don't want to bang the drum for religion, but I think at least a spiritual life, a spiritual approach to life really changes the way you look at things. It changes the way you look at women, it changes the way you look at family, it changes the way you look at children, and it puts them at the center of your heart and at the center of the business of being a human being. We have to stop talking as if stuff is all that matters. We have to start talking to each other as immortal souls, because that's what I think we all are.

Marcus Kowal

MMA FIGHTER, FOUNDER OF LIAM'S LIFE FOUNDATION

FOR ANY DAD THE THOUGHT of losing a child is something your brain almost blocks out. You can't even go there. It is something that I wouldn't wish upon my worst enemy. It is a pain that no human should have to experience.

After my son was killed by a drunk driver, I met a lot of parents, a lot of fathers who years down the line were still very angry and still very bitter. I wanted to help them, because two and a half years after my son died, and even though I live with a scar on my heart that will never go away, I can truly say that I lead a happy life again. A lot of times fathers will turn to drugs and alcohol, and that's not something that I condone. But I can understand it because you become so desperate to find a way to numb that pain.

Pain and grief are very subjective. There are certain things that are universal, and you have to find an outlet. I found mine by serving others and helping them. That's why I wrote my book, because this isn't something that you learn in school. You don't learn how to deal with grief.

What do you say to a father or a friend who has lost a child? How can you be there for someone? People told me all the time, "I don't know what to tell you!" and that is understandable. One of the best things I read was "What can you do for me? Can you give me my son back? If you can't, just walk with me until I face my demons and until I can see color again." That's very true. You can't do much, but you can be there for a friend. As a good friend, if you truly want to be there, then go over to their house, bring food, and tell them to eat it while you watch them eat it. Go for a walk with them. Just do something and be there. That means more than people understand.

Maybe they won't thank you then because they are lost in their own head, but that's the best thing you can do. If you are a parent who loses a child, try to find someone else who has been through it and come out on the other side and is happy again. Those dads helped me get through, and I do believe the book that I wrote, *Life Is a Moment*, which spells out the name of my son Liam, can help a lot of people both on how to deal and how to be a good friend.

Mike Lindell

FOUNDER OF MY PILLOW

I HAVE A BOOK OUT titled *What Are the Odds? From Crack Addict to CEO*, and it was a journey of a lifetime. God was always chasing me. I would tell my friends that we had to quit this stuff and share stories from the Bible I read while in jail, and they would quit, and I kept going.

It got to January 16, 2009, and I didn't have any money or any material things left. I knew that day that if I waited another day there would be two choices, reel A of the next part of my life or reel B. I knew that with reel A my calling would be gone. So was it a bottom? I guess it was a choice at that time, but I knew I couldn't go another day because things were going down a dark path or, with God, all things are possible.

My prayer that day was that I would be free of the desire to do drugs. I woke the next day and my desire was gone. Two months later, I went to a faith-based treatment center, and I learned a lot about why I was an addict in the first place. It all went back to my parents' divorce, the fatherlessness. I don't believe addiction is something you are born with. I believe it comes from stuff in your childhood. From either fatherlessness, father wounds, trauma, or one of those things.

Those going through addiction right now need their hearts restored. I was saying during the pandemic that if you are an addict that has made it through, now is a great time to reach out to your friends of the same age and same addiction, because they look for common hope. You can reach out to them and witness to them. They are looking for hope and living in fear. Especially during the pandemic, what a great time to get them set free.

If you are an addict sitting at home and can't get to a faith-based treatment center, reach out to someone your age who has made it through. That's your hope match. Get to somebody close to your age who was abusing the same drug and ask them, "How did you make it through?" We could make the pandemic the greatest AA meeting in the world using Jesus Christ as our higher power. People look for hope when times are bad, and we need to take away that fear and fill it with peace and hope.

I. V. Marsh

LEAD PASTOR OF BCOMING.CHURCH

IN ORDER TO GET CHILDREN to put God first in their lives, the father of the home 100 percent has to model it. It can't be a philosophy, it can't be an idea, it can't be something that we do on Easter and Christmas or just a blessing we say before supper. It has to be a part of the father's lifestyle, because children will always mirror what their parents live out as important. If you truly value your relationship with God, it will be passed down to your children as long as they see it modeled. In order to get my kids to model their life after God, I have to model it in my life and do it publicly so they can see and let them stand for things that should be stood for and give a voice to things that need a voice.

One of the reasons I believe God has been removed from so much of society is because I think as society moves on, they are trying to get rid of personal responsibility. I think the Bible puts a lot of emphasis on personal responsibility, so I don't think they like that. I think we are living in a world where people want to excuse themselves from their own actions and blame their problems on a plethora of things. That could be upbringing, race, zip code, handicap, learning disability, or it could be a ton of things that make us not want to take personal responsibility for our own progress in life.

All of those things cause us to push away the ultimate creator of the Earth and all life on Earth. I think from Genesis to Revelation, it really does speak to a God that created everything and made a way for you to have a relationship with me through Jesus. But the truth is it's your choice, and your choice has a cause and effect. So you need to take personal responsibility for your actions. There's a proverb that says that a man does foolish things to ruin his life and blames God in the end. We can't blame God for our own unwise decisions.

Chris Norton

KEYNOTE SPEAKER,

AUTHOR OF *THE SEVEN LONGEST YARDS*

I SUFFERED A SEVERE spinal cord injury playing college football, and I was given a 3 percent chance to ever regain feeling or movement below my neck. That started me on a journey. I had a strong foundation of faith. Just having that faith background and a belief in having hope was really instrumental, because I didn't know what was going on. I just had a strong belief that I could bring it all together and make this mess into a message and give this pain a purpose.

That was instrumental, but what else was instrumental was my family. My dad, mom, sisters, and the community of people just came pouring into me and encouraging me. My parents set the example that we were not going to let this injury define us and that we were going to live a full life despite the challenges we were dealing with, that we weren't going to dwell in the past. We were going to focus on what we could do today and in the future.

That was big for me—taking ownership over my life and responsibilities—and I got that from my parents. They didn't throw a pity party for me or complain; they were just doers. They were upbeat and positive, and that is how I wanted to be too.

My experience led me to meeting a beautiful woman named Emily, and four and a half years after my injury we walked across the stage at my college graduation. The video of that went viral and was seen over three hundred million times. We got married and I walked down the aisle at our wedding. We became foster parents and eventually began adopting our kids.

I now do speaking engagements where I have the opportunity to share my story. I am really blessed to be in a role to help other people and to motivate other people and give them hope. My mission now is to spread hope and change people's perspective.

Chad Prather

HOST OF *THE CHAD PRATHER SHOW*

I FIGURED OUT EARLY ON that when my kids were young that I wanted to teach them values. A lot of times we want to teach them right from wrong. Well, right from wrong can be different in different situations. Sometimes you can get those gray areas where everything isn't just black and white. So I say that if you teach them values, teach them to value the right things, then when it comes time to make those decisions, they will make them according to their values. If they do that, then typically they are going to make the right decision, because they don't want to choose against their values in situations.

Thankfully, I have five kids that have really lived that way, and it has enabled us to be able to have a big family and still pursue careers. When we are together, its quality time that we spend together, and we always make the time to be together. It's a juggle, but we have finally gotten it down to a science.

I think the phrase *toxic masculinity* gets tossed around quite a bit, and there has been a war on traditional masculinity. Masculinity to me doesn't mean that you have hair on your chest and you're a brawny guy and chop trees down for a living. Masculinity is a mindset, and I believe toxic masculinity is an oxymoron. If it is toxic, it is not truly masculine, and if it's masculine it's not toxic.

I want my kids to be who God created them to be, and I as a father want to be strong enough to help them determine that. Parents should have a wider field of vision and should be able to help their children and guide them so that their focus in life is used for good, to help make them the best they can be.

Erik Rees

FOUNDER OF TEAM NEGU
AND THE JESSIE REES FOUNDATION

THEY DISCOVERED A TUMOR IN our daughter Jessie's brain stem. Only about three hundred kids a year get this type of tumor; it's very rare but it was inoperable and incurable. It was the most devastating news my wife and I ever heard that our child has cancer and we had twelve to eighteen months with her.

She began writing messages, putting stickers on brown paper bags. She wanted to put her Beanie Babies in the bags to give other kids who couldn't leave the hospital. The hospital had to approve of this, and they had a few restrictions. One of them was that she couldn't use paper bags, so she needed to find a different vehicle. Jessie's middle name was Joy, so *Joy* and *jars* just went perfect together, and she started Joy Jars.

Back then we would make them in what was called the Joy factory, which was our garage. My job was to put the labels on the Jars, and her job was to stuff them. She had certain rules about how to make her Jars. For example, no cheesy toys and no air, meaning you had to pass the shake test. If you can stuff it so full that you can shake it and you don't hear anything, then that's a good Jar. If you could hear things move, then you can put more stuff in it. The first Jar she ever gave out was to a little boy named Christian.

She would visit other children's hospitals in Southern California. She couldn't go back to school, but she loved to write, so she started sharing her story on a blog on Facebook. CBS started to follow her story, and by the time Jessie moved to heaven, she had helped send Joy Jars to twenty-one different children's hospitals. Now we work with close to three hundred.

During all of this we held on to each other, we held on to Jessie, and we held on to our faith. When you are being blown, and the winds and the waves are hitting you very hard, you have to have something to hold on to. I would encourage people in similar circumstances to feel comfortable and confident in asking for help. We work with a lot of families now, and initially people don't want to ask for help because they see it as a sign of weakness. No, let people carry the stretcher for you and let people help. If you are getting bad news, whether it's cancer or other things, hopefully you are not alone and you have a community around you and relationships around you that can help strengthen you during difficult times.

Jason Schechterle

MOTIVATIONAL SPEAKER
AND SUBJECT OF *BURNING SHIELD*

FATHERHOOD IS FOR ME THE single greatest thing in the world. After my accident and having to spend five months away from home in the hospital and losing my eyesight, I had such an appreciation for just hearing their voices. I had a better understanding that these are lives that I helped create, and that is so much bigger than me. That is such a responsibility, and it's not their fault or responsibility for what happened to me, but it made me want to fight harder.

Then when my youngest was born, the way I look at that is it gave me a deeper appreciation of those who serve and the work that the firefighters did, the work that the doctors did and my tissue donor. They saved my life. I encourage everyone to be an organ and a tissue donor, because when I look at my youngest son, that is an entire life that was created because someone was willing to be a donor. If he grows up and has three or four kids, and then they grow up and have three or four children—it has no logical end. It can go on and on and on. When you put it into perspective like that, I just think it's incredible. That's why we are here—to leave something good behind. Leave the world better than you found it, and if you have children and you raise them right, then you can be proud knowing you're gonna do that.

Trent Shelton

FOUNDER OF CHRISTIAN-BASED
ORGANIZATION REHABTIME

I WAS RAISED IN THE church. My father was a pastor, so ever since I can remember faith has been a part of my life. But it was secondary. I always say that it was a part of my values, but I wasn't living it. I went to Baylor with a full athletic scholarship to play football. I spent three years in the NFL, but I was released and cut maybe about eight or nine times.

I hit a depression point and, really, a breaking point. I really started to look at myself and I realized I was talking it, but I wasn't living it. I had faith, but did I really have faith? Because my actions weren't reflecting the faith that I said I had. So I dived in deeper, and I got into my word and got into a better environment with faith-based people. My environment completely changed, and I needed to change my environment to strengthen my faith, and it did.

My old college roommate at Baylor committed suicide, and that really struck a chord with me. I really wanted to find a way to help people who were struggling and felt like life was over. From my struggle, I started RehabTime after my son was born, and I started sharing videos and messages online. I started helping people in the community, I started helping people online, I started helping people in schools, and that's what RehabTime is all about: really helping people turn their pain into power in any area of life. I want to do what I'm doing times ten. I want to impact more lives and help more people know that they're enough.

Ryan Stewman

WE ALL HAVE A PURPOSE in the back of our mind. God has planted a reason for us to exist on this Earth. Many people are out there ignoring it. Many are out there drinking it to death, drugging it to death, or sexing it to death. Many people are just trying to hide that voice, saying, "Shut up, voice, I don't want to be a motivational speaker. Shut up, voice, I don't want to go be an advertising guy. Shut up, voice, I don't want to be a sales guy!" Or whatever it is.

I can tell you from firsthand experience, when I started listening to the voice in the back of my head and finding the purpose that it was telling me all along, that's when things really took off for me. When I realized that my calling wasn't to be a sales trainer, it was to be a world changer—I realized this in 2005, and it took me eleven years before I even started to entertain that that was even possible. Now I think about how much further ahead I would be if I had started this process eleven years ago when it was first implanted in me.

You know what you are supposed to do. You know that you have a calling. You know that there is something that you're passionate about. You have a purpose, and the sooner you can get into that, the sooner your life will get into congruence with where you are supposed to be.

Kenny Thomas

THE DANCING DAD

WHEN WE FOUND OUT THAT our son was diagnosed with leukemia, the first thing I did was pray. I went into the room, I closed the door, and it was me and God, and that was it. See, what we do in private will dominate what we do in public. So we have to understand that God is not someone who is all out for display all the time. He's not impressed with likes and comments and all of this other stuff. It's your personal relationship from a faith level.

Then I went to my family, and we prayed together. That's what me and my family did. I prayed by myself as the leader. I needed to get the play call, and I needed to know exactly what we were going to do. We prayed around Christian before chemo even hit his body.

Then from there we went to the team of doctors and asked them what the play is. How are you guys going to treat this? I told them I wanted every single ounce of information so that I know exactly what is going into my son.

If you find yourself in a similar situation, the next thing you want to do is lock out any negativity. I don't care if it is from family. There have been times where we had doctors and nurses who had to be dismissed from our team because they had a bad attitude. It is very important because 70 percent of all diseases start within the mind. So if they start in the mind, we can end them with the mind. The medicine is something extra, but if you have a bad mentality, that is going to take over everything and medicine is not going to work.

It is important to have a positive mindset every single day. That's easier said than done, but you have to continue to motivate and talk to yourself. Pull yourself back from the situation and analyze the entire field and don't get emotional about everything. Again, that is easier said than done if your child is in a terrible situation, but it must be done.

You just can't be afraid to do the work. You have to put the time in; you have to put the effort in. Sometimes obedience requires sacrifice, but not all sacrifices are obedient. So if you look at it from that perspective, you're going to come out a winner on the other side.

Derrick Van Orden

NAVY SEAL VETERAN, ACTOR

MY FAITH HAS BEEN PARAMOUNT in raising my kids. It is at the forefront.

What is really interesting is that your children look at you as if you are the do-all-end-all as their parent, like you have all the answers.

But when they see you praying and understand that you have a faith and dependence in and on something greater than yourself, that really expands their mind. When they know you acknowledge that you *don't* have all the answers.

They start to understand that we are all part of dominion and it helps them get along better in life.

As individuals and as parents, when we look external to ourselves, things often turn out better because when we are self-centered or choose to rely solely on our own counsel we lose sight of the fact that it is not about us, it is about them. Them being our family, and it being life.

There has been a breakdown in our understanding of this in our culture at a fundamental level that is having dramatic and horrific effects.

For instance, a police officer should not be killing civilians, but then again, civilians should not be killing police officers. It's a two-way street.

When you have not grown up in a family system that is familiar with dominion, meaning that there are figures that have authority over you, and you respect those authority figures, these types of tragic events are logical extensions.

Many civilians do not understand or acknowledge that the police officer has legal authority over them and unfortunately, sometimes the police officer does not understand or fails to acknowledge that the reason they have been given authority over the civilian is to *protect and serve* them.

I believe this is a direct result of the breakdown of the most basic unit of society: the family.

We need to get back to traditional family values and structures. I hope one of the positive outcomes of the response to the COVID crisis will help with that.

I think there are a lot of moms and dads who were forced to stay home with their kids and realized how much they enjoy spending time with their children.

Maybe they will try to figure out a way to live without two incomes. If we could get back to the family structure of mother staying at home and dad working or dad staying home and mom working, I believe we will be so much healthier and happier as individuals, families, and a nation.

Tommicus Walker

OWNER OF WALKER ENTERPRISES

THE NUMBER ONE VALUE I hope to instill in my kids is God. I want to make sure that they understand and have a relationship with God like I had growing up. I grew up in a single-parent household with my mom, who raised me and my two older brothers. I just really want to instill those family values and make sure we are all close knit. I want them to understand that we are all we got. I want them to treat people how they want to be treated. The same principles that I've learned in the Bible.

I try to do that and emulate that in my life right now. God has to be at the center of everything. He has to be at the front, at the end, and also in the middle. Once you do away with that, it becomes chaos. So we try to pray every single day as a family. We try to eat dinner every day at the dinner table together as a family. Once my kids go to sleep at night, I tuck them in and make sure that we pray, because tomorrow is never promised to anyone. We want to make sure that we have that close relationship with God as we go through this journey called life.

Darren Woodson

NFL VETERAN SAFETY,
THREE-TIME SUPER BOWL CHAMPION

WHEN I GREW UP, MY MOTHER—she had four kids and I was the youngest—the way she kept us off of the streets and away from all of the gangs and away from all of the drugs and all of the violence was we went to school, to church, to the YMCA. The school bus would always drop us off at the church. The stopping point was the church. My entire foundation has been around my faith and prayer in God. That's the way I am built.

The one thing that I have always wanted to instill in my kids is faith and that they can always pray. I always tell people one thing: my job is just to manage my kids, because these are God's children. I just manage them through the process and try to guide them along the way. But God has His own purpose for my kids. As a father it is my job to get up every day, pray for them, and try to put them in the right positions to try and help them with their lifestyle and whatnot.

I can't be a control freak. I know that they're going to have their own things that they are going to have to go through. They need to see my face and see that I am supporting them and seeing that I truly believe in them. That just inspires so much confidence in them, and I can see it on their faces. I know what my purpose is, and I know what changes I've had in my kids' lives. When I'm positive and I'm confident and I'm supportive, then the outcome is always going to be good.

Fatherhood Ambassadors

FAR TOO OFTEN I hear dads warning other dads about future undesirable circumstances by using the stern cautionary phrase "Just wait until . . . [fill in any age or milestone event]." If your child is one, they'll forewarn you, "Just wait until the terrible twos!" If your child is learning to crawl, they may come at you with, "Just wait until he starts walking!"

Nobody hears these warnings more than the soon-to-be father. Just wait for the sleepless nights, the diaper changes, the feedings, the teething, and of course, the ultimate grave proclamation: "Life as you know it is over!"

For some reason, many seasoned or even new dads themselves seem to take pride in these warnings to new or about-to-be fathers. However, I find these statements to be the most misguided counseling a father can bestow. I do believe that most of them mean well, but this rite of passage does more harm than good. Men who are about to become fathers are already on edge about the transformational life experience that's taking place. Instead of the prophetic jargon about ominous events, I urge you to offer a more accurate phrase of encouragement, such as, "Life as you know it is just beginning!"

There is a fatherless crisis in America, and part of this is due to the various crises men face—such as imprisonment, suicide, military deaths, murder, and homelessness—that can lead to them being absent from the home. And statistics indicate that fatherless homes have a tremendous negative impact on children: 63 percent of youths who commit suicide are from fatherless homes. Almost all homeless and runaway children—90 percent—are from fatherless homes. And 85 percent of all youths in prison come from fatherless homes. Taking all of this into consideration, the last thing we should do is discourage new or about-to-be dads in any way.

On the other hand, we dads have the unique opportunity to be ambassadors for fatherhood. A word of encouragement at the right time can mean the world to a fellow dad. If a dad is waiting in line at a store and his baby is crying and whining, instead of rolling your eyes or shaking your head, you can make funny faces at the kid, to try and distract him or make him laugh. If you're at a restaurant and there's a family with a baby or young child, go over to the dad on your way out and tell him he's doing a great job, and compliment him if his kid is well behaved. When your friend or relative is about to become a father for the first time, save the war stories and instead tell him how much you love being a dad. These types of actions may not seem like much, but they can go a long way for a dad who may be constantly doubting himself.

Divorce and separation are other major factors that result in men walking away from their responsibilities as a father. Especially in these instances, the dad needs to be encouraged and supported to stay involved and active in their child's life. Difficult divorces and toxic relationships can create circumstances in which the dad makes decisions out of anger. We can remind anyone in this type of situation that just as we can't see our reflection in boiling water, we shouldn't make decisions while we're angry. Boys need their father. Girls need their father. We as a society need fathers. As the number of involved fathers increases, those horrendous statistics mentioned earlier will come down. And the benefits to our communities will be substantial.

I have spoken about the fatherless crisis at length with many of the dads on *First Class Fatherhood*. You're about to read words of encouragement from dads who have been divorced, dads who have started programs to help other men, and dads who grew up without a father and who have helped fatherless kids. If we truly want to leave this world better than we found it, let's leave it with fewer fatherless children.

Mario Armstrong

EMMY AWARD-WINNING HOST OF *NEVER SETTLE*

I THINK THERE ARE TOO many young men who are afraid of fatherhood and may want to avoid it. I think the problem is . . . I don't think we have done a really good job—I say we as in the media—about communicating the process. I think the *First Class Fatherhood* podcast is a part of the solution set for this. We don't really communicate the process. We just say that we became dads and life changed. We don't really discuss the process and the stuff in between before we were dads and after we became dads. It really just jumps from one to the other. I think a lot of what is really special gets missed right there.

The other thing that I think young people can be responding to is they are constantly getting bombarded with images of parents that are now not about their own dreams; they decided to check out on that and put everything possible into funding or assisting or supporting their kids' dreams. I think when you see an overwhelming picture that kind of shows that trajectory, that if you're getting to that age where you're thinking about having kids, you better hurry up and get what you want to accomplish in life because you're not going to be able to do it once you have kids.

When you kind of get fed that line over and over again, it's easy for you to start believing that that is the case. So I think that having podcasts like *First Class Fatherhood* and seeing other people that are more accessible on Instagram—like The Rock, who has really been awesome about showing his family and being revealing about his family and his upbringing but maintaining the fact that he is still driven and pursuing goals, and that doesn't mean that he is going to be less of a dad because of that. So those examples can help, especially for young people who are very impressionable.

Justin Baldoni

DIRECTOR, ACTOR, FILMMAKER

ONE OF THE REASONS I'm in the business I'm in is to be a part of changing the way men are portrayed in various roles—fathers, husbands, partners—in the entertainment world. Being a father is a gift, and the importance of being a father extends beyond the typical "financial provider" narrative that we've been fed. The most important thing we can provide as fathers is our presence. The same goes for our marriages and partnerships. How do we portray marriage in the media? The whole idea of the old "ball and chain" and the shit we men talk about, that's gotta go. The idea of having a bachelor party that's centered around having all the fun you can before you can't anymore because you'll be locked down in marriage, it's all bullshit. We've sensationalized these ideas and created narratives about how men are supposed to act or not act, how we should feel, or more importantly, not feel. And for the most part what is portrayed isn't aligned with who I believe most of us are at our core. From the conversations I've had with men all over the world, most of us don't desire the fleeting feelings of perceived or performative happiness. Most of us desire sustained joy, contentment, and meaning. That comes from connection—true connection—with others and with ourselves. That comes from being willing to be comfortable in the uncomfortable. It's about being willing to admit what you don't know and being able to reach out and ask for help. Too many of us men don't understand that it is okay to not know, it's okay to ask questions, to reach out to other men and ask for help. One of the biggest myths of masculinity is this feeling that we have to do it alone. We do not have to do it alone. In fact, in order to show up as the kind of fathers and partners we want to be—the kind of men and humans we want to be—we need to do it together.

Dean Cain

ACTOR, EMMY AWARD-NOMINATED PRODUCER

I WAS ADOPTED. My biological father split before I was even born. I was adopted by my father when I was four years old, and he has been such an unbelievably positive and wonderful mentor, role model, and father to me. It's incredible. I realized where I could've gone without that sort of parenting. He is a very different father than I am, but he was so unbelievable that I named my son after my father. They share the same name.

My son's mother and I weren't married when we conceived, and we weren't meant to be a couple. I wanted to be a strong, present father. Unfortunately, I had to go to court and fight for custody. I don't think it was set up to be particularly evenhanded. It took about fourteen months and over a million dollars in legal fees for me to win joint custody of my son, which I did. I've had full custody of my son since he was about nine. I am completely committed to my son, and I love being a father. My son is my favorite person to hang around with and travel with. We are super close as a result.

Being a single father is difficult, and the hardest part for me was balancing work and life. You hear a lot about that with single mothers, much more often than you hear about single fathers. I've been doing this as a single father for over eighteen years, working, doing all the work, and raising the child.

I changed my work to the effect that I wouldn't accept a lead role in any series because you are gone eighteen hours a day. That would've required me to be an absentee father, and I refused to do that. I wouldn't take any series that shot outside of Los Angeles. I had to turn down *Band of Brothers,* and I also turned down a series that shot in Canada—which would've made me one of the highest-paid actors in television—which ran for many years. We were there ready to sign, but it got killed because I would have to fight a move-away case with my son, and my attorney didn't think I could win that. So he basically told me I had the choice to make all this money and have this great series or be a father. So I chose: I'll be a father, no problem. It took me about a millisecond to make that decision.

Lou Dobbs

HOST OF *THE GREAT AMERICAN SHOW*

I THINK WE NEED TO strengthen our nuclear family units in this country, and that's a very complicated issue on one level and on another so simple. Neither party, Republican nor Democrat, although both talk about family values, actually live up to them. We need to have both parties committed first and foremost to the traditional American nuclear family.

What we really need is to have an understanding for every piece of legislation: What will be the economic impact on the American family and what will be the impact on those children of those parents in the American family? How can we do as much as we can to assure that media, Hollywood, our school systems, our corporations are working to make sure we have a wonderful environment for all of our children? I can't think of a more important issue for all of us to think about and to act upon every day and to put it in that light. I think what *First Class Fatherhood* is doing is extraordinary and wonderful, and I commend Alec Lace for what is a much-needed service to the country.

James Buster Douglas

FORMER UNDISPUTED HEAVYWEIGHT CHAMPION

I WOULD SAY IT'S THREE-TO-ONE fatherless kids who come into my gym. There is a lot of that, and it is unfortunate. A lot of these boys need guidance, and a woman can only show them so much. I've seen a lot of strong women come in here with their sons, and they are tough on them. But it's not like having a father. They do a great job of working with their boys, their sons, but there is a lack of fathers, and that is unfortunate.

I hate to see that because I grew up with a father, and I know how wonderful that was having him to look up to, talk to, and get advice from. My heart pours out to those young men who grow up fatherless.

We try to make the best with what we got. I run into guys that were boxing with me as an amateur who grew up without a dad, and they looked at my father as a father figure. How much he helped them—I didn't even know about it. I didn't know that was going on, and I was right there. My dad had respect and love for these young men. We lived in a tough part of East Columbus. It was a tough area in the city. To this day they say great things about my dad, because of the men they have become because of my father's influence. That brings a warm feeling inside to hear that my dad helped them out so much.

I try to do that for the kids that come into my gym, and I tell them even if they don't fight good, they are going to look good because I get them the best gear and nicest uniforms. At least before the bell rings, they'll look intimidating.

John Finch

AUTHOR OF *THE FATHER EFFECT*

THERE ARE A NUMBER OF people who have a way of thinking that suggests that most kids don't need a dad. Some Hollywood females in the last several years have spoken about surrogates and how a dad is not needed to raise a child. It is tragic and it saddens me to think that they have that viewpoint.

Every child deserves a father. What a mom can say to a child is totally different than when it is coming from a dad. To hear the words "I love you, I believe in you, I'm proud of you"—it means something totally different coming from a dad as opposed to coming from a mom. Every child needs that from a father.

I think that the younger generation is starting to get it. There was a report out by a sociology professor at Brigham Young who was talking about how fathers are more involved with their children's lives now than in the past. I think it is an awareness thing. More and more dads are becoming aware of the significant lifelong impact they have in their kids' lives. Instead of us beating dads up, and all of the feminists just going off about dads and putting them down, we need to be encouraging dads and lifting them up. We need to show them and give them the practical tools by which they can be better dads. I truly think most men want to be great dads; they just don't know how because it wasn't modeled for them, because their father wasn't there or maybe was abusive.

It was recently brought to my attention that we didn't even have a national holiday for fathers until 1972, and yet Mother's Day started in 1908. It goes to show you how society and the world view fathers, and it is very unfortunate. But it is something that we are motivated to change.

Jon Gosselin

REALITY TV STAR OF *JON & KATE PLUS 8*

I'VE BEEN GOING TO COURT for twelve years. It's not an easy battle. I've been through nine attorneys and spent at least $1.3 million in court back and forth with everything else. I ended up with two of my eight children. There could be more to come in the future. It's a long battle, and I just didn't give up. I'm still not going to give up.

It's not just "Wham bam, it's gonna happen." Everyone's court case is different, every state is different, and laws are different. I've just never given up. I go to court once a month, and it's getting better now that the kids are getting older. We do have a guardian ad litem, so it's like having a third parent. If there is a dispute between mom and dad, they can always call the guardian ad litem. She is a representative of the court and the judge, so she can make a better decision if there is a dispute, which has changed everything.

If you are a dad who is in the beginning stages of going through a divorce, take a deep breath. Little baby steps every time, and try not to take on too much at once. Because, guys, we are horrible at multitasking. So try to focus on one goal and try to get that goal done and then move to the next goal. When we try to take on too much, you're never going to accomplish the first step, and then you are going to miss out on certain things.

When you are spending time with your kids, make sure you are focused on your kids, and try not to get distracted so much because that can easily happen. For instance, with Sunday football, instead of going out to watch the game with your friends and your kid, just watch it at home when you have custody. Have your friends come over. That way you have control over that situation. If you go out and watch the game, you are never going to have control over that situation, and you will be distracted. The following Sunday when you don't have custody, then you can go out with your friends and do all those things. There will always be more football games, but your kids will only be young once.

Tony Hawk

SKATEBOARDING LEGEND

FOR DADS ON THE ONSET of a divorce, coparenting, or in a blended family, my best advice is just to stay present, don't give up, and sometimes you have to fight for it. You can't just leave it up to your kid necessarily by asking, "What do you want to do?" or "What about next Wednesday?" It's like, set a schedule and stick to it. I have noticed that, especially with my youngest, if I just leave the decision-making or the schedule up to her, she is not going to choose stuff that we're going to do together or choose to be with me. She needs that schedule and consistency. So, the best advice I have for that is to just stay consistent.

Be ready, be present, and push through the challenges of what seems like elements that aren't gonna allow you to be with them. Because you gotta keep treading water. You have to stay with them. It's worth the effort. That's the bottom line, and sometimes it just seems like an uphill battle all the time to make time or to get a schedule going. You just have to find it and stick with it.

That's what I've learned through this crazy year we've had with the pandemic. Because my schedule was more consistent in terms of travel—there was no travel—I realized how helpful it was to a couple of my kids when they knew that every Tuesday or Wednesday or Friday we're going to do something together. Whether that was going out to eat or see a movie or something, that consistency really helped them with their mental health too. As a dad, everything is going to change. It's going to be exhausting, it's going to be challenging, it's going to sometimes seem impossible, but it's all worth it.

Nick Hoffman

SINGER, SONGWRITER, AND HOST OF *NICK'S WILD RIDE*

THE HARDEST PART ABOUT DOING what I do for a living is being gone. I am a very driven guy. I'm almost a workaholic. That drive suddenly gets very much diminished when you know that you're missing out on time with your kid.

I am acutely aware of the fact that my daughter is very young, and the best years of her wanting me to be around to hang out and these cool discovery moments—they are going to go by very quickly. So being gone for two weeks filming in Africa, for example, suddenly isn't as much fun when you know you are missing out on stuff at home. And couple that with the fact that I don't see her as often as some people see their kids anyway because we live in a divorced scenario.

I have been divorced from my daughter's mom for most of my daughter's life. I am remarried, and her mom has a fiancé that has been in the picture almost as long; so I don't see my daughter as much as I would like. I have to make the best with what I've got when I've got it. That is a challenge in itself—with Skype calls and phone calls and all of those things. You have to stay accountable, and you have to stay present. It doesn't matter if you are on the rode in Africa or you are right down the road. It is difficult when you have those types of scenarios.

I am really lucky. We are really lucky, because it really takes a village to raise a child, and I don't have her 100 percent of the time. Her mom and her fiancé have her for the majority of the time. There is definitely some difficulty going between households, but we have made it as easy as possible. We are lucky because we are amicable, and we are able to communicate. We definitely coparent as a foursome.

Don't get me wrong; it has its difficulties, but our daughter never sees them. When something that requires some disciplinary action with her does come up, we get on the phone with each other and tell each other here is what she did and here is what I said so that when it comes up there is a consistent message. I think that is so important. I think the most important thing that I have learned about being a divorced dad and in a coparenting family is about maintaining that level of communication and trying to overcome your insecurities and trying to overcome your jealousies and trying to overcome all of these things about your divorce and just make it about the child.

In the end it is about giving the child the happiest life possible, and my entire goal has been to keep the peace so that by keeping the peace we can communicate, and by communicating we can be better for our daughter. I would be lying if I said that was easy. There have been times when my ex's fiancé and I have squared off, and the girls have had some uncomfortable stuff. But cooler heads prevailed, and they prevailed because we were able to communicate and coparent. In our case, our daughter is surrounded by four people who love her.

Conn Iggulden

COAUTHOR OF *THE DANGEROUS BOOK FOR BOYS* SERIES

BOYS DON'T MAGICALLY KNOW HOW to tie knots and do woodworking and fix things they break around the house. They have to be taught. They have to learn, and perhaps they have to learn that they have to learn. They need to be taught that as well.

If you look at some of the famous figures in history who lost their fathers at an early age, they ended up with a sort of ruthless ambition that might have been good for making empires but wasn't that great for themselves. I'm referring to people like Genghis Khan, who lost his father at about the age of eleven. Julius Caesar was I believe about thirteen. When my son was thirteen, I jokingly told him if he wanted to go out and conquer the world, the best thing I can do would be drop dead right now.

The point is if your father is around, he can show you a version of masculinity that involves patience. My dad was a very patient man. One night he was helping me with a math project that had to be in the next day, and I was practically in tears because I wasn't getting it. My dad was extremely patient with me and stayed after it until well into the night, and that really taught me something.

A father's love is very valuable, and when it is missing from the world, we all know about it. We need to promote fatherhood. Without a father figure you can get sort of a polarized male who can easily be all about violence and gang life, because without a father figure, he will form his own role models in the wrong places. Boys are going to look for role models, and they will take them wherever they can get them.

A big part of the male psyche is he has the ability to laugh at something terrible, the ability to be kind and make a stupid joke even when it's a really dark thing that is happening. That is a big part of the male psyche and the human psyche. You need it.

Michael Irvin

NFL HALL OF FAME WIDE RECEIVER

I LOVE TO SPEAK TO FATHERS. It's one of my passions. Speaking about the fatherless issue that's out there, the fathers who are not on their post. Right now in this country we are about 33 percent Caucasian Americans having babies out of wedlock, where the fathers are not there. Fifty-two percent Hispanic Americans where the fathers are not there. We're about 73 percent African Americans where fathers are not there, and it has a devastating effect on kids.

So that's why, as a father, if you're a father out there and run into a father, you gotta try and encourage the father. I don't care where he is in his relationship with his kids. He needs to get back to it even if it's estranged. Don't let the relationship between you and the mother get so bad that the kid has to suffer. Even if you have to, I don't condone divorce, but if you have to go get a divorce from the wife, you should never ever divorce the kid. Stay on your post no matter what. That's our jobs as fathers given to us from the Father. Stay on your post!

Carlin Isles

WORLD'S FASTEST RUGBY PLAYER

MY THING IS TO ALWAYS be consistent. Consistency is everything. You can't do things only when it's convenient. You have to learn to work through issues regardless of what it is. My ex and I always had a great relationship, and now we are coparenting. I always wanted to make sure that she was fine and that they were fine. In that type of situation, it's not about you, it's about them. My thing is always looking out for each other in the best interest and not being bitter. Whatever the situation is, if you are bitter, then that is when everything goes downhill. I always want the best for people, and I don't want there to be any bitterness in the heart.

Communication is the key to understanding and just love in general. Regardless if we are together or not, there is a level of respect that we have for each other as parents of our kids, and that's what helped us a lot in our situation. It is tough. Believe me, it is tough. You have to keep things in the forefront and the right perspective, and that's the key.

John James

UNITED STATES ARMY VETERAN, APACHE PILOT

THE NUCLEAR FAMILY AS WE traditionally know it creates a sense of otherness for folks who may come from broken homes. That's why I believe it has been portrayed as something that is obsolete. I absolutely think that is wrong. I do believe, and science will even show, that the most successful children come from very strong, stable, successful nuclear families.

I talk all the time about my values, faith, and family. I truly believe that the foundation of this country, the infrastructure that we are neglecting the most, is the strength of the family. When you take a look at the most successful children, again, they come from the strongest, most stable families.

I think that we need to start portraying families in a more positive light. I think that we must start getting men to step up and not shirk their duties and take care of their kids. I think we have a fatherhood problem in this country, and we need to address that. We need to do everything that we can to get people the resources they need to take care of their families and address their issues. I think that until we address the issues with broken families in this country, we are going to be going around and around in circles. Because you can't replace family with food stamps. You can't replace parents with programs. We need to make sure we are growing our kids into responsible, contributing adults. The best way to do that is to make sure that we have healthy, strong, and functional families.

Struggle Jennings

COUNTRY RAPPER

WHENEVER I AM ON TOUR, after I sing my song "Like Father, Like Son," I say, "Gentlemen, go home and raise those boys to be men." It's the biggest problem we have in our country right now—the lack of fathers and leaving all of that pressure on women. Women are so strong and can do so much, but a boy needs a man.

I was away for five years in prison, and I had to kind of find my role. I couldn't just jump right in and ease my way back and be there for them and let them know that I was back and that I wasn't going to mess up again. There's a level of trust that comes into play.

I tell the crowd every night, as I try to guide guys back to their families, that children are resilient, and they are forgiving and to go be the father that they need you to be. I plan on running around and screaming as loud as I can about this. There may be some emotions in the beginning, and some will have their arms wide open.

My children have taught me about unconditional love. That's been my biggest integrity check—like who do I want my son to be? What kind of guys do I want my daughters to date? I have to be that guy. I can't sit here and raise children and do the complete opposite of what I want them to do.

We all want our kids to be better than us, so we have to do our best to be our best. You have to guide your children to be the best they can be and the kind of people that this country needs. I know that so many people get caught up feeling like "What if I'm not a good dad?" Just be there and be the best dad that you know how to be. When you have a child, you never have to worry about being alone because you will always have someone in your corner. Children always love their fathers, even when we don't deserve it sometimes.

Alexander Kane

ACTOR AND PRODUCER

I HAD AN ATTORNEY AND A JUDGE tell my ex-wife if she just kept fighting enough that I would do like most fathers and throw my hands up in the air and walk away. Well, she found out that wasn't the case. We have been going on a ten-year battle, and I am as active as I was then in pursuing the best course of life for all of my children. But they do make it feel like you are fighting an uphill battle.

Essentially, one of the things that made me want to become an actor was I felt like this next generation full of guys did not have the male role models. It is okay to be a tough, testosterone-filled male that kicks ass with one hand and treats women and children kind with the other hand. We are missing those Paul Newman, Robert Redford, Steve McQueen kind of actors these days. If they are not in the home, they need to be on the screen.

I set out to become an old-school Hollywood icon. Not the male chauvinist, but to show boys who didn't fight world wars and don't have a male role model to look up to that on camera and off camera you can watch a guy that can be tough, can be proud and full of testosterone, to be not afraid to say what he thinks and won't back down in the face of social pressure. A guy who says you are not going to make me feel guilty for being male or for being anything other than myself. I am going to be that guy on camera, off camera, and I am going to be a great dad, a great husband, a great friend, and a great humanitarian.

That is what I set out to do, and when I go into an audition, that is what they get. They get Alexander Kane 110 percent, and if they don't like it, then I don't need their role. So far it has worked out pretty well, because I find that while Hollywood tries to soften men, the public is actually still thirsty for these types of male role models.

Aaron Lohman

RETIRED NYPD SERGEANT

I BECAME A COP OUT OF NECESSITY. I didn't think that I would ever be anything, and it was because I grew up in a single-parent household without a dad. I didn't have any encouragement. I didn't have anybody to teach me how to be a man, and I really had no idea what I was doing. I was just kind of floating through life, and I can definitely see that happening in the neighborhoods that I work in also. I did the same thing. You look toward the person that is a year older than you to be your male role model. Meanwhile, they're growing up and doing the same thing as you, and that is what leads to a lot of gang activity.

People want to be part of a group. They want to belong. They look to that person who is older than them who isn't necessarily doing the right thing. Then they're buying guns and selling drugs and engaging in gang activity. Then the younger kids see that, and they think this is normal, and it leads to a cycle of unfortunate violence. We have to help these kids break these cycles, because they don't know that there is any other way out.

Don't listen to miserable parents, because being a dad and being a parent is awesome. It's a learning process. I hate it when other dads say to each other, "Oh, just wait." Some parent will be saying something like my kid is great and they say, "Just wait until they're one," or "Just wait until you have a second one." It's like they're setting you up to feel negative about being a parent. Don't listen to negativity. Just enjoy being a parent and spread that message of how awesome it really is.

Ryan Michler

HOST OF *ORDER OF MAN* PODCAST

THERE ARE SO MANY BOYS who are growing up without father figures. If you look at the rates of fatherless homes, it has increased. If you look at the number of women in teaching professions—our teachers are mostly women. So boys aren't really getting an example of what it means to be a man. That's why they are not figuring things out, because they aren't being taught from other men.

A lot of society would say that you don't need to be taught how to be a man by a man, but that's the furthest thing from the truth. Masculinity is bestowed, manliness is bestowed; it has to be learned, and it has to be learned through other men. The most infectious thing we can do is set the example for our families as fathers and husbands and then also reach out into the community as well.

That's why it is so important that I coach teams. I look at the boys that I'm coaching, and some of them have great father figures in their lives and others don't. It's critical that I step up and extend my hand beyond the walls of my home and into the lives of these boys who may not have a father or father figure so they can understand what it's like to be a man and how a man shows up in his community and his family and his business and every other facet of his life. At the end of the day, it's just about being the example and sharing what it is and showing the world what a good man looks like.

We have to live it ourselves. We have to push ourselves outside of our comfort zones. If we don't do anything scary or tough, then all our kids will see when we come home from work is how we complain about work, how tough work was. Then we sit on the couch and drink a beer and watch the game and not engage or do anything hard with our lives. Our kids will think, "Okay, that's the way it is supposed to be." Rather than a guy going out, waking up early and going to the gym and kicking ass and doing everything he needs to do, putting himself in challenging situations and coming out not unscathed but coming out all the same.

The more you can exemplify that and show it to your children, the more they will see "Okay, this is the operating system for life." If you don't want your kids to grow up and be weaklings, then don't be weak. Go out and grab life and live it the way it is supposed to be lived, and your children will do the same. It all starts with us. It's about teaching them, yes, but are you doing it yourself? If you are doing it yourself first, then all the rest of this stuff will fall into place.

Titus O'Neil

WWE SUPERSTAR

IN THE BLACK AND BROWN COMMUNITY, the fatherless problem is very detrimental. It determines a whole lot, to a lot of kids, to not have that male role model in the home. I was raised by a very strong mother. Based on my childhood and not growing up with a father or a male role model in the home that I could look up to, I always knew that if I was going to be successful at anything, it would definitely be being a father. It's a role that I always wanted to be in, and becoming a dad helped me embrace my manhood.

The only thing my mom could never do was teach me how to be a man. I think there are same-sex homes that are raising successful families and being able to make things work in a positive way. There are single parents who are doing amazing work. But to me, as far as my life was impacted, there was always a mentor or a coach. A lot of them were males, and they served as kind of father figures to me.

For years there has been a stigma for some women that they don't need a man. Well, they do. Eventually, they will at some point because there needs to be a male and female influence on everybody's life. Everybody can't have a motherly touch, and everyone can't have a fatherly hand. We all need that. We all need people we can grow with and talk to that lead us in the right direction to become the best human beings that we can possibly be, and I think that males and females can both do that. Being able to help rear a child in the right direction is a big responsibility, and the best way I can do that and illustrate that is by the way I live and the way I walk and talk.

Chris Santillo

AUTHOR OF *RESILIENCE PARENTING*

WE ARE ALL A PRODUCT of our environment and a product of our upbringing. We all have to forge our own path. I lean heavily on the resources all around us. I must have read a thousand parenting books before my kid turned one, just looking for knowledge. Some things resonate and some things don't resonate. There is a lot of information, but not everything works for everyone.

You just have to reach out to the people around you and be comfortable having what I would sometimes consider awkward conversations with other dads about their own parenting and how they are raising their kids and what the results are. All of our experiences are largely anecdotal until we get to a larger pool and find someone who has a different experience. I was speaking with someone recently who has one child that is three years old. This dad was having certain challenges, and I very gently offered some things that he might want to consider: every kid is different, but here are some things that I have found to be successful with the thousands of kids I have worked with over the years.

He said, "Oh well, no, no, no. That's not the right tactic." I said, "Well, maybe try it on for a little while and give it a go and see how it works or if it resonates with you before you dismiss it." There is a lot of wisdom out there, and we can all be better parents. It's the strive and drive to be a better parent every day that opens up our potential.

Brendan Schaub

UFC FIGHTER, PODCASTER, AND STAND-UP COMEDIAN

IF YOU ARE ON THE FENCE about having kids, or you know a guy who is on the fence about having kids, let me say this: I've done a lot of cool shit in my life. I've played in big major division one football games, the Big 12 Championship. I played in the Mile High Showdown against CSU multiple times. I have been on some big cards fighting in the UFC. I have done sold-out shows doing stand-up comedy. I have done a lot of cool stuff. Nothing, nothing compares to being a dad. Nothing even close, man. On a day-to-day basis, there is just nothing like it. Take advantage of it and embrace it. There is nothing better. I know it's cliché to say this, but I am telling you, man, I have done a lot of cool shit in my life and there is nothing better than being a dad.

Curtis Sliwa

FOUNDER OF THE GUARDIAN ANGELS

IT IS SO IMPORTANT THAT KIDS have a healthy respect for their father. More importantly, the father is able to teach the son and the daughter what they should and shouldn't do and set an example.

For instance, my father was a merchant seaman, and you would've thought he would drop the F-bomb every second word. But I only heard him use the F-bomb one time in my entire life. He went out of his way to make sure he was a good example. He didn't smoke, he didn't drink, because my grandfather became a lush later in his life. So my father wanted to make sure me and my two sisters did not go down that road. He observed a certain regimen. My father understood that we were watching him. He was our father figure.

My mother was obviously the hen that ruled the nest, but my father always made sure he walked that straight and narrow path so that it wasn't, do as I say but not as I do, which is unfortunately happening in a lot of households. The kids look at the dad especially, and they say, "Look at him, he's a degenerate gambler, he's chasing skirts, he's bending his elbow, he's smoking cigarettes, he's doing doobs, and then he's telling the kids they can't do it." Parents have to realize that. Mothers do it a hell of a lot better, but fathers have to understand that it's not *I* and *me*, it's *us* and *we* when you have a family. Even if you are on the outside looking in, even if he can't live there any longer, you still have to set an example, and not enough men consider that, I think, when raising their children.

Eric Snow

FOUNDER OF THE WATCH D.O.G.S.

WE CAN'T SAY TOO MANY great things about dads and their roles in our kids' lives. Something that is very near and dear to my heart is Watch D.O.G.S. (Dads of Great Students). This is a program that schools bring into their own school, run it with their own parents, with their own teachers, with their own faculty. But it really reaches out to the fathers and father figures of their students and invites those men to take a full day off work, come into the school, and spend that entire day working as a volunteer at the school as a Watch D.O.G. as a dad of a great student.

We want each guy to do one day. If we can do that and get a different dad there every day, that's a great thing. There's about 180 school days in the year, and the average school has about five hundred kids, so the math works. A lot of schools are able to get a different dad there every day because of this program.

So many universities have done studies about the important role that dads play in their children's lives. Fifty years ago, the dynamics were such that in the typical family, mom stayed home, and she was the caregiver and homemaker, and dad went out and earned a living. That has changed, as now over 70 percent of moms are working outside the home as well. Dads are changing diapers, dads are going to the store getting groceries, moms are taking the cars in for a tune-up, and it's all about coparenting.

Schools are sort of lagging behind that message that dads have an important role too. Maybe the schools aren't lagging behind; it's the dads who are lagging behind believing how important a role they have in their children's lives. Typically, when schools invite parents in and volunteer, mom feels the social pressure to make the time to come in and volunteer. That pressure is placed on her and her alone in most cases.

The dads kind of skate. Nobody tells us to be a homeroom parent, nobody is telling us to bring in snacks for the group. So by schools bringing in a Watch D.O.G. S. program, the school lets the dads know they are talking to them and not just to the moms. As dads, if we want to be viewed as active, engaged parents, if we want to be viewed as a parent that also can be nurturing, that we want to be included in these things, we have to be the change we want to see.

Shawn Stockman

SINGER, SONGWRITER, BOYZ II MEN

I DO THINK THERE ARE way too many kids growing up without a father in the home, and it is leading to many of the problems in our society today. I've had friends of mine that might not have taken care of their kids as good as I thought, in my opinion, that they should have. What I tell friends of mine, and even other fathers, is what we miss as dads.

Let's be honest, when it comes to most of the disciplining and stuff like that, the mother does most of it. There's a role that we all play, and it's not old-fashioned, it's not misogynistic or anything like that. We all play roles, and every role is different. The one thing that is constant is that all kids need to see, and this is psychologically how important this is, just to know that their father exists. I would tell my friends just be there. Just be there. Like even if you don't do anything and you just sit on the couch watching the games or taking a nap, the kids can look while they're running around acting up and say, "I have a dad." Just that, knowing that they have a connection to a male figure, does wonders for their psyche. When you are not there, it has the opposite effect.

So I tell a lot of guys out there who may not get along with their wife or mother of their child or whatever the case may be, it still doesn't take you away from your spiritual presence in a kid's life, and how much that helps their development for them to know that they have a father around. That is one of the most important things that kids could ever have in their lives.

Danny Trejo

HOLLYWOOD ACTOR AND RESTAURATEUR

I REMEMBER WHEN MY KID'S mom remarried, and she had two kids on the spectrum. Her husband left, and my son was trying to do whatever he could, and then I took over. Because that's his mom. That's the thing we must remember. That's our kid's mom. So I stepped in to do whatever I could. My son said to me, "Dad, you're raising the bar pretty high to be a good dad." I'll never forget that. I've never forsaken my kids, no matter what I felt with their mom; that doesn't matter. They always know—and they have to know—that their dad is there, no matter what. You gotta be there, and that's all. A lot of us aren't good with relationships and marriage, but kids are forever. So when you're having kids, get ready for the joy of your life. It doesn't matter what relationship you have with the child's mom. Don't ever let your kids see you mad. Don't ever let them see you angry at her. I did that. I remember when my three-year-old son asked, "Dad, why don't you move downstairs, so you and Mom won't fight?" So all that affects them. Just make sure you know, above all else, that's the mother of your children.

Benjamin Watson

NFL VETERAN TIGHT END, SUPER BOWL CHAMPION

THE FATHERLESSNESS ISSUE IS A very serious and important topic. Fathers obviously serve a role when it comes to provision and protection. They also play a big role on an emotional and sociological side. Fathers are protectors of a child's emotions. They are providers not just of physical needs but of emotional needs.

Fathers are protectors. They protect the child from physical threats outside the home. They protect their children from those who want to bully them or those who want to take advantage of them.

They are also the prophet in the home. When I say "prophet of the home," I mean that they are the spiritual leader. The man is the spiritual leader of his household. That's not to say that a single mother or the wife has no role. No, she has a role equal to that of the man, but when it comes to order, biblically, the man is the spiritual leader. The father is the priest of his home. Biblically speaking, the priest is the one who goes before God on behalf of his family covering them in prayer and leading them when it comes to understanding and worshiping. The role of the father is vitally important.

When you really break it down, you can see how when you remove the father, then chaos ensues. Again, that is not to say that a mother who is a single mother can't do a great job, because she can. But even if you talk to her, she will say it would be great if there was a guy right here that was helping me. Because kids statistically have better outcomes when they have a mother and a father in the home.

Also when it comes to dads, not all dads are perfect. But a father is for many of us, or for all of us, the first idea of what our heavenly Father is like. That was much of the weight and responsibility I felt when I had my first child. I know that I am going to fall short, and we all are. I am his first or her first idea of what it means to be loved, what it means to have a hero, what it means to have someone love them unconditionally. That's what a dad does, and so dads are vitally important for the family unit.

But also when you talk about society as a whole, they are important when it comes to that. When you look at fatherlessness, it's estimated that a third of our kids are growing up without a dad now. In order to address fatherlessness, we have to challenge men that they have what it takes. Whether you had a dad or not, you have what it takes to be a great dad. It is already in you, and we believe you can do it. Also, you are needed. We need you to step into that role. If you are married, great, that's preferable. If you are not, you can still be involved, and we need you to be involved.

We need to encourage men that they can do it because a lot of society is telling men that they don't have what it takes. That they are going to be aloof, that they are going to be distant, they are going to be ill prepared, and that they just can't do it and they have no expectation to do it, and we expect them to run around and do a bunch of different things. That's what society is telling them. We need people to tell them, "No, man, we encourage you: you can do it, and we need you to do it."

It is a huge issue, and it is something that if we don't take care of it and if we don't address it in a multifaceted fashion, both personally and in society at large, then our kids don't really have much of a chance.

New or About-to-Be Dads

ONE OF THE first questions a reporter often asks a player who has just won the Super Bowl is, "What does it feel like to be a champion?" A common reply to this question is, "I'm really not sure—it hasn't hit me yet."

This can be true of fatherhood as well. The anticipation of having your first child is overwhelming. Everyone in your circle feels obligated to give you advice and tell you how you're going to feel. Your partner has carried the baby for nine months and is going through labor pains. She is on another level of the first-time parent experience. One thing you're certain of is that your life is about to change, and with change comes discomfort.

Father of eight Wayne Dyer once said, "If you change the way you look at things, the things you look at change." So your expectations of what fatherhood is all about are important. One of the many reasons a new dad may have a bad experience is because of what he's expecting. Maybe he was given bad information by one of his friends who had a negative experience. Maybe his perception of fatherhood has been altered by his own experience of having a bad dad. Whatever the reason for having low expectations as a new dad, this can impact your personal experience of becoming a father.

Other factors can play into your experience of becoming a father. My own journey to fatherhood began with a bit of trepidation. During my wife's first full-term pregnancy, we went through genetic counseling. This is a process in which doctors review your family history and run a series of blood tests. It just so happens that my wife and I are both carriers of cystic fibrosis, a condition that affects the cells that produce mucus. It is rare, and according to the Cystic Fibrosis Foundation, there are approximately one thousand new cases of cystic fibrosis diagnosed each year.

That my wife and I are both carriers meant there was a one-in-four chance that our child would be born with this condition. The news was alarming, especially since we'd suffered a miscarriage with our first pregnancy. The hospital strongly suggested we have an amniotic fluid test, to determine whether our child was positive for cystic fibrosis. We quickly refused the testing, since there was nothing we could do in the event our child was positive. We left it in God's hands, and we have been blessed with four children, all of which tested negative.

As you read the advice from the incredible men in this chapter, I'd like to offer some of my own. Many of the dads I've had the honor of interviewing on my podcast have served in the military. They develop a service-before-self mentality, which carries them through the most difficult situations. The first time I ever experienced this type of mentality was after I become a father. Having a child will unlock a part of you that you never knew existed. It will awaken a feeling in you that has been sleeping your entire life. The feeling that will awaken in you is fatherly love—the feeling of loving someone more than you love yourself. My advice is to embrace this feeling and allow it to make you a better man. Allow it to transform you into a first class father.

At the end of each interview on *First Class Fatherhood*, I ask my guest to offer some advice for new or about-to-be fathers. These are some of their answers.

Morten Andersen

NFL HALL OF FAME KICKER

LISTEN TO YOUR CHILDREN as they grow, because they give you honest feedback. Have patience in the early years, which can be frustrating because you can't communicate with a newborn, and they can't communicate with you, although they are trying. Take the journey with them, watch them grow, and enjoy the process. Impart wisdom that they can use.

The job of a parent is to prepare your kids to be self-sufficient, independent thinkers. The greatest gift you can give as a parent is the gift of wisdom and levity. Give them those tools, those commonsense tools that they can take with them when they leave the house. Of course, they are going to make mistakes; we all do—but that they learn from them and they have enough in their arsenal to go out and be productive, happy, passionate human beings in society.

Troy Brown

BODYBUILDING CHAMPION

YOU HAVE TO BE A man of integrity. You have to remember this: you are either moving forwards or going backwards; you can't stand still. You have to consistently grow your mind as a man. You want to be healthy, and you want to have that health consciousness, which is going to be a great environment for your children to see.

If they see their dad crushing it, hitting goals, and he is moving in the right direction, he's reading, he's working on his mind, he's putting the right foods into his body—you will just become this badass father that your children see. You become their hero, their role model, their superhero. You become this governor man that everyone around you—your wife, your kids, and the rest of your family—is so proud of.

But in order to get there, there's gonna be ups and downs, and that's life. It's the ups and downs that will make you more resilient and allow you to be stronger as a man. It's there to test you, and it's there for a reason, so don't crumble away and back away from it, face it head-on and take ownership and make a decision that you just gonna go all in. Everything starts with a decision; transformation starts with a committed decision. When you decide to go all in, that's when you know you are never going back to your old self.

Grant Cardone

CEO OF CARDONE ENTERPRISES, CARDONE CAPITAL, FOUNDER OF 10X MOVEMENT

THE ONLY ADVICE I HAVE for anybody is be the best person you can be. Forget being a great dad. If you're not a great person then you can't be a great dad. Don't be a great dad. Be a great person! You can't be a great dad if you're drunk. You can't be a great dad if you're tired all the time. You can't be a great dad if you're making excuses. You can't be a great dad if you're broke and worried about money every single second of the day. I know because I've been all those things, and I was good to no one when I was worried about those things. If you're not taking care of your physical condition, you can't be a great dad because you won't live long enough to be a great dad.

So I would say, don't be a great dad. Be a great person, whatever that means to you. There are only a few categories that we're all interested in: health, finances, relationships, charity, or whatever those handful of things are that make you feel good—be great at those things, and it'll probably transition into you being a great dad.

Robert Creighton

BROADWAY ACTOR—*FROZEN, CAGNEY: THE MUSICAL*

WHEN THINGS ARE HAPPENING, you can ask your kids or yourself as a dad, is it a big problem or a little problem? I would say remember that question. I ask it when something sounds very dramatic to my five- or seven-year-old. When the world seems to be coming to an end and there's a meltdown happening, I'll say, "I understand that you're upset about that, but is it a big problem or a little problem?"

The same thing you can say to yourself when you have a child or you're about to have a child and you're stressed about things and you don't feel prepared or whatever. Ask yourself, "Is it a big problem or a little problem?" Ninety percent of the time or 95 percent of the time, in the big picture, the answer is it's a little problem. So it's not worth the stress or anxiety that you might give it. You can tell yourself that you can get through it because it's a little problem.

There are big problems, of course, and health issues that you need to address. But generally a lot of things that you think in the moment are big problems, if you step back and ask, "Is this a big problem or a little problem?" the answer is often that it is a little problem, and that may help you move through it a little more easily.

Trent Dilfer

NFL VETERAN QUARTERBACK, SUPER BOWL CHAMPION

ROUTINES ARE REALLY IMPORTANT. I think it's important that you and your wife have a routine, and a young child has a routine. I think that obedience is very important. When my daughter was sitting in her high chair and she would knock over her baby food, I would take her out and I'd walk her up the stairs and put her in the crib, and she would cry. I'd sit by the door, and when she stopped crying, I would get her and bring her back down and put her in the high chair.

She would eat a little bit and then knock it over again, and I would pick her up and put her in the crib again. I would do that over and over until she understood that the first time she knocked over her food, she would be disciplined. Eventually she stopped knocking over her food.

That's important because if your child is at the park and they start running toward an intersection and you yell "Stop!" would they stop the first time, or do they hear your voice as just a suggestion? I don't want my voice to be a suggestion to my kids. I want my voice to be the primary voice in our kids' lives.

Having routines and having obedience has really helped with that. To this day, if we say something, the kids trust it as the primary voice in their life. They don't always have to agree with it now because they are older, but they still recognize it as the primary voice. I think a lot of that is because we didn't give suggestions. When we spoke to them, they knew it mattered.

Ramon Dominguez

HORSE RACING HALL OF FAME JOCKEY

I ABSOLUTELY LOVE MY JOURNEY as a father. It's not an easy thing, especially when the kids are like my kids approaching the teenage years. They are getting a sense of independence, which is normal, but at the same time I feel like I have learned to become a better listener. Instead of always dictating and saying, "Well, this is the way it is!"—there is a time and a place for that; however, you can also try to put yourself in the shoes of the kids and look at life through their eyes and come to a common ground.

One thing that I learned recently is when I tell them to do something and they give a little push back, I'm open to telling them they can change the rules if you give me a good reason. Sometimes they come back with a great explanation or a great argument, and I say, "You know what, we can do it that way." So it doesn't have to be black and white. We can definitely come to a gray area where we can communicate and negotiate, and it is great and something that is enjoyable. No one, regardless of how young they are, and they are supposed to listen because you are their father, no one really wants to be told all the time what to do. So it's great when there is this common sense of respect and understanding.

Heath Evans

NFL VETERAN RUNNING BACK

WE STARTED WHAT I LIKE to call vitamin N, which is vitamin "no," very early with our kids. Kids don't always need to understand why they are being told no; they just need to learn to accept no because they will be told no a whole bunch of times by parents, teachers, and coaches. And we need to teach our kids how to handle being told no with a good attitude.

More importantly, we have to teach our kids how to say no to themselves. When they are in those situations where the kids around them are drinking or participating in drugs or maybe a boyfriend is pressuring them into a situation that they know they're not supposed to be in, being able to tell themselves no—no, you can't do that; no, you can't have that; no, you can't partake in that—is huge power. In our society kids are growing up and they don't know how to handle being told no, and they definitely don't know how to tell themselves no.

I tell my girls every week to trust the process. I'm raising you in such a way that you will dominate this world in fifteen years because you guys are growing up in a generation with a bunch of kids who can't discipline themselves, can't be told no, can't tell themselves no, and don't know how to push themselves through physical and emotional and spiritual pain. There are fewer and fewer real leaders being raised, and I am bound and determined to raise two loving, kind, dominant, powerful women that don't need to tell the world that they are powerful, because when they walk in a room, their presence demonstrates power.

Ben Gardner

KANSAS HIGHWAY PATROL
TROOPER POPULAR ON TWITTER

SLOW DOWN AND RECOGNIZE what you have in front of you. I think about how fast I moved and how I was always just trying to get to that next moment. If it was just getting to eating or cleaning up or just getting to the event and when the event was over with— just slow down and take it all in and recognize that these moments are gonna pass, and you're not going to have them anymore because your kids are going to grow up fast and you are going to miss them.

I reflect, as most parents do when their children are older, you look back at your children's pictures of when they were babies and when they were newborns. When they get older, you're thinking, *Man, I miss them days.* New parents don't recognize the wonderful moments they are having. I know they are difficult, because there's a lot of heavy lifting you have to deal with when it comes to a newborn. But they are some great times, so slow down and embrace the moments and look to extend the moments, not to just move forward and get to the next task that needs to get done.

A. J. Hawk

NFL VETERAN LINEBACKER, SUPER BOWL CHAMPION

YOU CAN TAKE ALL THE classes you want. I took all the Lamaze classes. I took the classes where I had to put diapers on fake babies and all of that. Once you have your child, your instincts take over and you just figure it out.

You can be worried, and you should be kind of worried and anxious. I still get like that when my wife travels. She's an interior designer, and she's been traveling a lot recently. Whenever she's not here, I have all four kids. When they go to sleep, I get worried at night for them. All of a sudden, the responsibility of all four kids kind of hits me, because she's not there to bounce stuff off of, and it's just me. I roam the house and check on the kids while they are sleeping. My oldest is eight, so I probably shouldn't be doing that anymore.

You should read everything you can, and you should want to be a great dad, but you figure it out as you go. One thing I do is when I see people who have kids that are well behaved and I respect the parents, a lot of times I'll ask them, "Hey, what are you doing? I notice your kids are so well behaved." They will tell me one or two things that they've done that has helped them along the way. I try to take little things like that from parents I respect and try to implement some of that in my daily life.

Bedros Keuilian

FOUNDER OF FIT BODY BOOT CAMP

SOMEONE IS GOING TO RAISE your kids, and it might as well be you! Here's what I mean by that: I make an attempt to have one-on-one conversations with my kids anytime I can, whether that's outside in the backyard shooting pellet guns with my son, or my daughter and I are taking a ride to get some yogurt. I'll have the type of one-on-one conversation with my daughter where I'll say, "Hey, honey, I'm going to open the door for you to go inside, and in the future when you grow up and you have a friend, who is a boy that you like, and you go on a date, like Mommy and I go on a date, if this boy doesn't open your door, like I open Mommy's door and your door, you turn right back around and come home or you call Dad and I'll come pick you up."

And so I have these conversations in times where it's not threatening, when we are in the car, or we are out in the backyard. But I am instilling core values in my kids. That's what I mean when I say someone is going to raise your kids and educate your kids. They are either gonna become modern-day knights and active members of society, or they're gonna become entitled little brats if society raises them. Because, unfortunately, society says, "Hey, you should depend on the government, you should depend on the man, and it's someone else's responsibility." So I instill values in my kids because I don't want anyone else raising them.

Jason Khalipa

WORLD CROSSFIT CHAMPION

NO ONE HAS IT ALL figured out. You can read every book you want, but at the end of the day, every child can be different, every situation can be different, and that's okay, that's the fun in it! Don't stress yourself out with these social pressures, but do what you think is best for you and your family. Sit back and ask yourself, "Am I being a good dad? Am I doing the best I can?" and if you can answer that with a yes, then you're on the right track. I think that's really important.

I also think at the same time you have to look at yourself in the mirror, and if you're being a dirt bag, you have to tell yourself that. That's not okay. You have to be there, and you have to hold that relationship with your wife super strong so that you guys can have a strong front to raise the kids. I think also a key element is to not forget about date nights with your wife and things that make you feel like you're dating again, which I think carries over to the kids.

Marcus Luttrell

NAVY SEAL VETERAN AND *NEW YORK TIMES*
BESTSELLING AUTHOR OF *LONE SURVIVOR*

IT'S A PROGRESSION, and no matter what seasoned parents tell a new parent, you are still going to default to your own parenting regulations of what you see and what you learn. It is all trial and error.

Everything literally changes when you become a father. Sleepless nights, yeah those do exist; you just have to get used to them. You'll eventually get into the zone. It's kind of like going through hell week. Just know that people have been going through this and parenting since the beginning, before they had hospitals and all that stuff. Have a great time with it because it does go by fast.

Don't ever be embarrassed or ashamed to not know something. Ask around, ask for advice, and don't be afraid to adopt something that somebody else does that is working. As the father, you need to realize what your woman just went through with carrying that baby and giving birth. I watched my wife give birth to our children, and I was like, women are the toughest people I've ever seen—and I know pain. Take on the diaper duty and the night shifts and be involved.

Max Martini

HOLLYWOOD ACTOR—*SAVING PRIVATE RYAN*, *PACIFIC RIM*

WHAT I REALLY TRY TO do as a father is try to eliminate any kind of gap between my age and my kids' age, without losing my place as being a role model. I try to really listen to them at their level and try to understand the things that they're going through as kids or as teens.

I think a lot of parents get stuck in this sort of disciplinary, parental space, and they lose communication with their kids. So for me what was really important is trying to remember where I was at that age and what I was going through. It really helped me in terms of having patience with my children and trying to give them solid advice. I go back and think, what I would've wanted to hear going through the exact situation, because I know there was a moment where I was in the exact same spot. That will open up a lot of good communication between parents and their children.

And get lots of sleep when they're young. My wife and I had our kids on a military nap schedule, and it saved us. We had friends who would ask us how we were getting so much sleep, because our kids would sleep twelve hours at night. It comes down to having a routine; kids benefit from having a routine.

Ryan Michler

HOST OF THE *ORDER OF MAN* PODCAST

YOUR JOB IS TO RENDER yourself obsolete. Your job is to put yourself out of a job. There are too many parents out there who think we're supposed to be buddies and friends with our kids, and everything should be happy-go-lucky all the time. But that's not true. At the end of the day, your job is to give your kids, your boys and girls, all the tools, skills, and skill sets to be able to go out in their life and make something of it and not necessarily need you.

I want to be wanted by my kids; I want to be involved in my kids' lives even after they've moved out of the house. I want to be part of their experiences as they go out and start their own families and start their careers, and of course I want to be part of my grandkids. But at the end of the day, I want to be wanted, not needed. So my goal with fatherhood is to remember that my job is to render myself obsolete. Sometimes that means I need to approach things from a friendlier perspective, and other times it means I need to be a little tougher and take a hard-line stance on some things so they can have the tools they need to thrive. It's not always comfortable, and it's a challenge—probably one of the most challenging things I've ever done—but it's also hands down the most rewarding thing I've ever done. So my job is to put myself out of a job.

Ed Mylett

ENTREPRENEUR TOP 50 WEALTHIEST UNDER 50

YOU NEED TO BE THE example that you want your children to become. There is nothing that you will do with your time that is more valuable than spending it with your precious children. When you get to the other side, and your children are older like mine are, you will regret the moments you didn't spend with them.

If you have to work three jobs, that's wonderful. But let me just give you some advice, brothers—when you're home, be present! When you are home, you have to be present, you have to engage with them, you look them in the eye, and you spend your time with them. I don't think being a dad is about the amount of hours you spend with your kids, but I do think it's about how important they feel when they are with you, and that when they are in your presence, they are the most important thing in the world to you. Nothing you will do, no words you will tell your kids, will replace the actions that you take in front of them. The one thing your kids want to be is the most important thing in the world to you and you do that by giving them your undivided attention when you're in their presence.

We are all busy dads, we are all trying to provide, we are all doing multiple things to put food on the table, we are trying to move our families forward. I know the mistake that can be made in all that hustle is that sometimes when we are home, we're not home.

We're on our phone, we're looking away, we're distracted, and we are worrying about our problems. Every time we do that, we are telling them that whatever we are thinking about is more important than they are. So, as a new dad, I would tell you, make sure they know that they are the most important thing in the world to you when they are in your presence.

Carson Palmer

HEISMAN TROPHY WINNER AND
#1 OVERALL NFL DRAFT PICK IN 2003

THE FIRST COUPLE OF YEARS of being a dad are so challenging. They were for me. If you're a guy who needs eight hours of sleep like I do, those first couple of years can be so difficult and so stressful. From the financial issues to the issues that come up between you and your wife, trying to nurture this kid and raise this new child and trying to be a good parent and trying to be a positive influence and all the things that come up—it gets so much better.

The first couple of years are amazing, but there are a lot of challenges. There are a lot of times where you are just tired and done and just want to get to bed. But it just gets better and better. Each month and each year, it gets better, from feeding them baby bottles to watching the first time they pick up a spoon and feed themselves. Seeing your child put on his underwear and get dressed for the day and then walking and running—it just gets so much better.

My opportunity of being a dad keeps getting better—all of those hurdles and milestones that you cross and all the struggles you have early with having a baby, they all make it so much better and enrich the opportunity of being a father so greatly as they get older.

The excitement of being a parent is unlike anything else, and it is challenging early on, but it is so well worth it and so enriching as you get older.

It's so exciting to see them start to play sports and doing well in school and going to your first parent-teacher conference and hearing positive things about your kid and also hearing the things that they need to work on, and the challenge of working on those things that the teachers may recommend and all the things that go with it are great. You just have to power through those first couple of years, especially if you have twins, and it will get better and better each year.

Dom Raso

NAVY SEAL TEAM SIX VETERAN

IT'S SO IMPORTANT TO MAINTAIN the relationship with your significant other. There are going to be changes in your life, and you need to be open-minded to the idea that life is going to change for you now. You need to embrace that and run toward it.

We like to say "Lead by example"; we like to say "Lead by our actions"; and we think we're going to be great. But kids will hold you accountable to that because the way they act and the way they respond is because you're doing it, you've made it okay. You may not see it because you have to take the blinders off; you have to be able to look at yourself. When kids argue, you say, "Why are you arguing?" and then you think, "Wait a second, I do the same thing." Now there is an element to that of making them understand that "I am the parent, and this is a safety issue and you have to listen to me."

I always try to give my kids the why, but leading by example is so important to live by. Assess that and really try to implement it and live by it and refine it every week and ask yourself, "Am I doing everything I can to lead by example, by my actions, by my example, by how I'm talking to my wife, by how I treat everybody in the family and other people?" Because they are watching, and they are taking it all in.

Being a father is one of the most important jobs in the world, and we have to take it seriously, and it has to be the number one priority. Your difference made in the world is going to be through being a great father and setting that example and knowing that there is no more fulfilling thing in the world that you could possibly do.

Jason Redman

NAVY SEAL, PURPLE HEART RECIPIENT, AND *NEW YORK TIMES* BESTSELLING AUTHOR OF *THE TRIDENT*

LOVE YOUR KIDS AND COMMUNICATE with your kids. At the end of the day, look at yourself. Be the dad you wish your dad had been, because I know there's a lot of people out there whose dad was not for whatever reason. Maybe you had an abusive dad, maybe you had a violent dad, maybe you had an alcoholic dad.

Everything about this life is built on choice. So many people convince themselves, "Well, I'm just gonna be this because of my demographics" or "because of my background" or "I'm related to this person, so that's who I am." That is a lie. That is a lie that we tell ourselves and you become pinned to the X inside your own mind. You have a choice, man.

So if you did not have a great father, be the father that you wish you had, and that starts with how you lead yourself. Take care of yourself with fitness, nutrition, sleep—that's all part of physical leadership. Be hungry for knowledge—that's all part of mental leadership. Control your emotions and don't blow up—that's part of emotional leadership. Kids are going to do dumb things; we all did. Accept it and love them for it anyway, and use it as an educational part.

Have social leadership by surrounding yourself with good people that your kids will look up to. Understand that the people you're around, your kids are going to emulate. The last part is spiritual leadership. Understand there's a big world out there. Follow those things and be the dad you wish you had, and I'll tell you what, your kids will grow up and be great.

Mike Ritland

NAVY SEAL VETERAN AND *NEW YORK TIMES* BESTSELLING AUTHOR OF *TRIDENT K-9 WARRIORS*

PUT IN THE TIME. Do the work. It's not easy; it's going to be one of the hardest things you've ever had to do, and it's for the rest of your damn life. You should take that responsibility as a privilege and realize that you are going to be the one, or one of, the key ingredients and influencers in that child's life to shape how they turn out. You don't have 100 percent control, but you play a big freaking roll in it, and don't take that lightly.

I'm not going to say don't screw it up, because you are gonna screw it up. Realize you're not going to do it perfect; you're gonna make mistakes. We're all human. Just like every other aspect of your life, learn from it and don't do it again. Use that feedback loop that your kids provide you with, constantly, to learn from your mistakes and make adjustments, and pivot when you need to if you're too hard on them or too soft on them, if you're too involved or not involved enough.

Always set the example! If you don't want to aid in the population of dipshits running around, don't be one. Set the example, put the time in, and be consistent and make it happen.

Matt Roloff

REALITY TV STAR—*LITTLE PEOPLE, BIG WORLD*

EVERYBODY HAS TO FIND THEIR own way. There's no real perfect guidebook to tell you to do it this way or do it that way. Let your kids be who they are going to be. Obviously, you want to discipline them and teach them manners and please and thank you and all that. But really, at some point you have to let go of trying to control your kids and forcing them to be somebody that they are not.

I have four kids, and they are all different personalities, extraordinarily different. They match all four corners of the world in terms of their thoughts and their beliefs and pursuits and all of that. I just have to love them and accept them for that and work to switch gears and develop them and realize that they all have different needs and desires from my time. I didn't always understand that perfectly, and it's cost me. I am finding that out and making good on some of those early mistakes.

But my biggest advice for new dads is let your kids become who they are. If they're into video games, then become a video gamer with them. If they are interested in reading, become an avid reader with them, or whatever the case may be.

Sid Rosenberg

HOST OF *BERNIE & SID IN THE MORNING* ON WABC

I CUT THE UMBILICAL CORD for my daughter, and I watched the doctor put my wife's large intestine back into her body after the C-section of my son. When you look down at your child for the first time, you're in love. You're in love. That is it. That's just the way it goes. It's hard to explain it if you've never been through it, but you're in love right away and at that point, you have to do what you feel is right.

There's no manual on this. I can't tell you, hit your kid or don't hit your kid, yell at your kid or don't yell at your kid, let your kid cross the street when he's nine or wait until he's fourteen; it's all up to the individual. I think that you fall in love on day one and you do the very best you can. I think most people are good parents, most people are loving, and most people have good intensions. Unfortunately, this is maybe the only thing in life where there is no manual, there are no directions, there's nothing to follow. You basically operate every day from the heart.

Craig Sawyer

NAVY SEAL VETERAN,

FOUNDER OF VETS FOR CHILD RESCUE (V4CR)

DON'T TRUST YOUR KIDS TO just anybody. A lot of predators work themselves into a position of authority where they have access to children. A lot of those are trusted official positions. Be hyper vigilant and look after your children. Try not to leave them alone with anyone if you don't absolutely have to, and try to minimize that exposure.

I'm a believer in security cameras that keep people honest. Try to realize that not everybody is as trustworthy as you'd like them to be, and so make sure you're looking after your little ones so that nobody shatters their little psyche when we think they are safe.

The child sex trade is the fastest growing criminal enterprise on Earth. In short order, if not already, it will be larger than the narcotics trafficking trade, and we all have a sense of how big that is. An estimated five million children are involved in this, and it is a $150 billion industry. The United States is one of the busier locations on Earth for child sex trafficking, so you have to be hyper vigilant of who you trust with your kids.

Vincent "Rocco" Vargas

ARMY RANGER VETERAN AND HOLLYWOOD ACTOR—

MAYANS M.C., RANGE 15

ONCE YOU PUT YOUR EYES on that kid and hold that kid, you'll know exactly what to do. You're going to protect that kid, and you're going to put that kid first. Be sure to keep that mindset of putting that kid first with every decision you make. Be relevant in your kid's life; don't be a paycheck. Show that kid love.

Don't ever be afraid to be the disciplinarian as well as the nurturer. You can be both. But what you don't want to be is too much of a friend. They have to always know that you're Dad. They have to know that you're always gonna protect them, you're always gonna do your best to give them the right direction and mentorship. As long as they know that, and as long as they feel loved, don't be afraid as a father to show affection. Give that kid a kiss. Give them a hug every dang day. Let them know that it is okay for a man to show affection as much as a woman. That is important for fathers to know.

Give that kid some strength and teach them to be a strong person and a strong leader in this community, because we need them. We as fathers are the mentors for tomorrow's leaders, and we need to make sure that we do that.

Robert Vera

BESTSELLING AUTHOR AND MOTIVATIONAL SPEAKER

TRY NOT TO TRAVEL AS much in the first three years. That would be my advice. Just hunker down and stay at home, because traveling, which I did a lot of with our kids, it's exhausting. Here's why: it's not like you're going on vacation, you're just taking everything you basically own with you, and you're just changing locations. Car seats and everything. It gets difficult.

It's an endurance game, so try to think long haul. Get as much sleep as you can. You won't sleep much, and that's the hardest part.

Being a dad is not as hard as you think it is because you are equipped with all the skills you'll need. It's not a scary thing. You just won't sleep a lot those first few years; so I would suggest that you don't travel too much in those first three years.

Kurt Warner

SUPER BOWL MVP AND NFL HALL OF FAME QUARTERBACK

THERE IS NOT A BOOK out there that is flawless in telling you how to be a parent, how to handle every situation, how to do everything right, and make sure you handle all your different kids with different personalities and all of that correctly.

One piece of advice I can give, and that I've always found to hold true, is regardless of how perfect or imperfect you are or how perfect or imperfect your children may be, the bottom line is every day make sure that they know that you love them. Regardless of where you missed it or they missed it, that it doesn't affect the way you love them, the way you feel about them, the way that you will go to bat for them in any and every situation. That's the bottom line in our family: our kids know that every day they are loved without question.

Their two greatest advocates are their mom and their dad in every facet and every way possible. We are not perfect, we have messed up and had to apologize, and they have done the same. But that doesn't make us waver in that unconditional love and the way we feel toward them each and every day.

I would say to any father out there, make sure your kids know that every time they go to sleep, every night before their heads hit the pillow, that there's never a question in their mind how much you really love them.

Allen West

FORMER CONGRESSMAN, ARMY LIEUTENANT COLONEL

I THINK THE MOST IMPORTANT thing is to close your eyes and think about the child you were and the relationship you had with your dad. If it was a good relationship, see how you can build upon it. If it was a bad relationship, learn the lessons and improve upon it. Because good lessons and bad lessons—they are all lessons that we have to learn from and go forth. And always tell your child "I love you" so that they never have to go anywhere else to seek that love that you can give.

Sean Whalen

CEO AND FOUNDER OF LIONS NOT SHEEP

NEVER LIE TO YOUR CHILDREN. Never lie to your children no matter if it hurts their feelings, no matter if it's a tough topic, if it's a dangerous topic, or a hard topic, don't ever fucking lie to your children to try and protect them. Always tell your kids the truth, even it's going to hurt their feelings, even if it's a difficult conversation. Never, never ever lie to your children.

And you can tell your kids how to be good kids, you can tell your boy how to be a man, and tell him to open up doors and say please and thank you, and tell him to have manners. But what are you showing them? If you want your kids to grow up and live their lives and live their dreams but you're working twenty-hour days, hating your life, hating your job, hating your marriage . . .

Something I firmly believe in is showing your children, especially our sons as a man, how to live life. I don't remember a lot of stuff my dad told me, but I remember what he showed me. I remember how I felt growing up. And when you stop and think about that—somehow as men we think that just by us living in a different era that's going to change. It's not going to change. We have to show our children what it is to be a man. We have to show them that masculinity isn't just banging on our freaking chests acting like we have every answer. We have to show them that shit is real. That we have emotions. So I'm very engaged in what my kids participate in and what they study, and I spend a lot of time with them.

Dana White

UFC PRESIDENT

WHEN YOU HAVE A BABY, it's always really hard in every sense of the word *hard*. You're not sleeping much, financially it becomes very tough, it's expensive. But it's the greatest thing you will ever do, and it only gets better. You will figure out the financial side, you will figure out time and sleep and all that other stuff. It just gets better every single day, and it's the most rewarding thing you can do in life.

There is never a right time. If you say, "I gotta wait for the right time!" there's never a right time. You just have to jump in with both feet and roll with the punches. It all works out and it will be the most rewarding thing you'll ever do in your life.

Josh Wolf

COMEDIAN

RELAX. PUT DOWN THE BABY BOOKS. All they do is put pressure on you and your kid, because you start to worry "Why isn't my kid doing this?" I remember when my son was in preschool and his friend, who was two and a half, wasn't talking. He was more physical than he was verbal, and the mom was going crazy wanting to know why he wasn't speaking like everyone else. I was telling her to relax, he's gonna catch up. If he's twelve and he's not speaking English maybe you should go talk to somebody, but he's way more advanced physically.

Relax, everybody. Just know that you're not gonna be perfect, because there is no such thing. The most important thing you can do is love your kid and let things happen. Don't make things happen. Let things happen naturally with your child and you'll be fine.

Acknowledgments

I HAVE BEEN EXTREMELY blessed to have been given the opportunity to speak with so many incredible men about a subject that is near and dear to my heart. I am thankful for every dad who has joined me on *First Class Fatherhood*. When my children are old enough to begin having kids of their own, they will have access to a treasure trove of conversations of their father speaking to all of these wonderful people about parenting, and that brings a level of happiness I did not foresee when I first hit the *record* button. My very first interview on *First Class Fatherhood* was with Eric Snow, president and founder of Watch D.O.G.S. (Dads of Great Students). Eric, I am grateful for you agreeing to come on a little-known podcast and share your fatherhood journey as well as your vision of the Watch D.O.G.S. program.

It wasn't until I was forty-seven episodes into the podcast that I landed my first celebrity dad to join me, and that dad was Superman, and Super Dad, Dean Cain. I genuinely enjoyed my conversation with Dean and was amazed by how openly he discussed his fatherhood journey. Afterward, Dean shared the episode on his social media accounts and by the weekend *First Class Fatherhood* became the #1 Podcast of Apple Podcasts Kids & Family category. Dean, I don't have the words to describe what your kindness, friendship, and support has meant to me over the years. It is no surprise your son Christopher is an outstanding young man. This world would be a better place if it had more dads like you.

My wife is a fan of reality TV, and a few years ago she suggested that I reach out to the dad and star of *Little People, Big World*, Matt Roloff. Boy, am I glad I listened. Matt, you are an inspirational man and a First Class Father all the way. Thank you for inviting me into your home on the Roloff Farms for our third interview. The fact that you have the longest-running family-focused reality television show comes as no surprise. Reality TV and TLC are blessed to have you and your family for so many years and I am blessed to call you a friend.

Now, I am often asked what is my favorite interview or dad that I have interviewed on the show. It is no secret that I am an admirer and supporter of the US Navy SEALs. I've now had the honor of interviewing over sixty frogmen on *First Class Fatherhood*. I have read almost every one of the books available about the SEALs. My absolute favorite is *Fearless* by Eric Blehm, about Navy SEAL Adam Brown. Being a recovering alcoholic and addict myself, Adam's story of overcoming addiction and many other major obstacles to become a member of SEAL Team Six really moved me. Adam died in action on March 17, 2010, in Afghanistan. I invited Adam's father, Larry, a veteran himself, to join me for a Memorial Day special edition and it was an interview I will always cherish. Larry became emotional, I became emotional, and I am extremely proud to live in a country that has produced people such as Larry and his family. May God bless you, Larry, and I pray that I am living a life worthy of your son's sacrifice.

Of course, I am a proud supporter of all branches of the military, and I would like to thank Connie Boucher for inviting me to cover the Medal of Honor Convention. Having the opportunity to spend time with and interview men who have earned their place in the history books has been the experience of a lifetime. Thank you, Connie, for an experience I will never forget.

I would like to thank the NFL for inviting me to several Super Bowl Media Days, which afforded me the chance to speak with Tom Brady, Patrick Mahomes, Bill Belichick, and so many others. I believe there is a need to see NFL players as more than just athletes—we need to see and hear from them as dads. I'll never forget the look on my son's face after Super Bowl LV ended and I told him I was going into my bedroom closet to interview the players virtually as they walked off the field. And while I'm talking about the NFL, I have to say thank you to First Class Father of seven Kurt Warner. Kurt, thank you for joining me twice on the podcast and sharing so much wisdom about your experience as a father.

Rita Rosenkranz, my literary agent, you were the answer to a prayer. From our very first correspondence on the phone, I knew you and I would have a wonderful partnership. You enhanced my vision for what this podcast would look like between the covers of a book. Your honesty, patience, and professionalism has been a comfort to me as we bring *First Class Fatherhood* to the bookshelves. Thank you for always being available when I needed you.

Amanda Bauch, Andrea Fleck-Nisbet, John Andrade, Jeff Farr, and the entire team at HarperCollins, thank you from the bottom of my heart. I have been a one-man band running *First Class Fatherhood*, and allowing access to this incredibly special part of my life is not an easy thing for me to do. I understand that doing all of this during a pandemic was new territory for all of you, but you made me feel comfortable from the beginning. Your communication and dedication throughout this process assured me that I was in good hands. One thing that you made perfectly clear is that red font on my computer is working very well. But your vision was synonymous with mine on every correction and suggestion.

My brother, Brian, I love you. You are the only family outside of Jess and me that our kids have in their lives. You are a First Class Uncle and have been a far better friend to me than I have deserved sometimes. You have a way of bringing humor to every situation, and my life is happier because you are in it. Thank you for always having my back and helping me to see things from a different point of view.

Aunt Dotsy, you were there with me through the darkest days of my life. Even as you were facing hardships and struggles in your life, you always take the time to talk to me at any hour of the day. You have been the biggest fan of *First Class Fatherhood* and I can never wait to jump on the phone and tell you who I booked for the podcast or what adventure I'm heading out on next. I pray to have a marriage as successful and beautiful as you and Uncle Jack's.

Christopher, Logan, Aiden, and Emily, you have made me learn more about myself than I could possibly ever teach you. God has given me the gift of being your father and it is a role that I will continually work on for the rest of my life. I can wait, but I look forward to each of you starting your own families.

Jessica, my love, we have come a long way from the stoop, and I honestly believe we are just getting started. The success of *First Class Fatherhood* would never be possible without you. There are times, especially in the early stages of this process, that I know I spent way more time on this than I should have. Thank you for understanding my passion and always rallying behind my overambitious ideas. Thank you for being such a great listener and a loyal partner. You are a beautiful person inside and out. I hope our kids grow up to be like you.

To all of the listeners of *First Class Fatherhood* and you, the reader, thank you from the bottom of my heart. I honestly believe that if we can strengthen the nuclear family units and reduce the number of kids growing up without a father or father figure, then the majority of our problems in this country will begin to evaporate. Please continue to tune in and spread the message of *First Class Fatherhood*. From the little acorn grew the mighty oak.

List of Contributors

ABRAMS, DAN
ABC Chief Legal Analyst, *New York Times* Bestselling Author

ANDERSEN, MORTEN
NFL Hall of Fame Kicker

ANKIN, DAVID
CEO and Host of *Toymakerz*

ARKO, JOE
Strength and Conditioning Coach

ARMSTRONG, MARIO
Emmy Award–winning Host of *Never Settle*

ARROYAVE, EDWIN
Founder and CEO of Skyline Security Management

ATLAS, TEDDY
Legendary Boxing Trainer

ATTAR, AUDIE
Founder and CEO of Paradigm Sports Management

BALDONI, JUSTIN
Director, Actor, Filmmaker

BANTON, GLENN
CEO of Operation Supply Drop

BELFORT, JORDAN
The Wolf of Wall Street

BELL, MARK
Professional Power Lifter, Inventor

BELMONTE, JASON
World Champion Ten-pin Bowler

BLEDSOE, DREW
NFL Veteran, Winery Entrepreneur

BRENKUS, JOHN
Producer, Director—*Sport Science*

BRENT, TIM
NHL Veteran, Real Estate Developer

BREWER, JACK
NFL Veteran Safety

BROWN, JEROME
Personal Chef to the Stars

BROWN, MATT
Professional UFC Fighter

BROWN, TIM
NFL Hall of Fame Wide Receiver

BROWN, TROY
Bodybuilding Champion

BUCKLEY, A. J.
Actor—*SEAL Team, CSI: NY*

BUSBY, ADAM
Reality TV Star of *Outdaughtered*

CAIN, DEAN
Actor, Emmy Award–Nominated
Producer

CARDONE, GRANT
CEO of Cardone Enterprises, Cardone
Capital, Founder of 10X Movement

CARMICHAEL, EVAN
Entrepreneur and YouTuber

CARTER, ANDY DANE
Real Estate Expert, Author, Podcaster

CARTER, NICK
Singer, Actor, Musician,
Backstreet Boys

CHONTOSH, BRIAN
United States Marine, Silver Star
Recipient

CLOTHIER, KENT
CEO of Real Estate Worldwide

CLARK, RYAN
NFL Veteran Safety, Super Bowl
Champion

CONDE, RAFA
DEA, Narcotics, SWAT Officer

COPELAND, ADAM "EDGE"
WWE Superstar

COPELAND, BRANDON
Professor of Financial Literacy,
NFL Linebacker

CRANE, ELI
Navy SEAL Veteran, Founder of
Bottle Breacher

CREIGHTON, ROBERT
Broadway Star—*Frozen, Cagney:
The Musical*

CSINCSAK, JESSE
Professional Snowboarder,
Entrepreneur, Winner of *The
Bachelorette*

DANEYKO, KEN
Three-Time NHL Stanley Cup
Champion

DAVIS, TERRELL
NFL Hall of Fame Running Back

DEEGAN, BRIAN
Most Decorated Motocross Driver in
X Games History

DE SENA, JOE
Founder of Spartan Race

DILFER, TRENT
NFL Veteran Quarterback, Super Bowl
Champion

DILLARD, DERICK
Reality TV Star, *Counting On*

DINNELL, J. P.
Navy SEAL Veteran

DOBBS, LOU
Host of *The Great American Show*

DOMINGUEZ, RAMON
Horse Racing Hall of Fame Jockey

DORIAN, SHANE
Professional Surfboarder

DOUGLAS, JAMES BUSTER
Former Undisputed Heavyweight
Champion

DUFFY, SEAN
Former United States Congressman,
Wisconsin

DURANT, MIKE
Nightstalker Pilot, POW, Battle of
Mogadishu

EAST, ANDREW
NFL Veteran, YouTuber

EFFERDING, STAN
Professional Bodybuilder and
Power Lifter

EVANS, HEATH
NFL Veteran Running Back

EYRE, RICHARD
New York Times Bestselling Author

FINCH, JOHN
Author of *The Father Effect*

FINK, MICAH
Navy SEAL Veteran

FLANSBAUM, SCOTT
Paralyzed United States Marine

GARDNER, BEN
Kansas Highway Patrol Trooper
Popular on Twitter

GIBSON, KYREN
YouTuber, Influencer

GOLDBERG, LEE
WABC-TV New York Chief
Meteorologist

GOSSELIN, JON
Reality TV Star of *Jon & Kate Plus 8*

GREGORY, LOUIS
Former United States Department of
Homeland Security Director

HAMPTON, BRANDEN
Entrepreneur, *Forbes* #1 Rated
Influencer

HANNITY, SEAN
Host of *Hannity* on Fox News
Channel

HANSON, GUNNAR
Navy SEAL Veteran, Pastor

HARDWICK, NICK
NFL Veteran

HARRIS JR., DAVID
CEO, Uncorked Health and Wellness

HARRIS, RYAN
NFL Veteran Center, Super Bowl
Champion

HARRIS, TYLER JACK
Sold Eight Thousand Life Insurance
Policies in Three and a Half Years

HAWK, A. J.
NFL Veteran Linebacker, Super Bowl
Champion

HAWK, TONY
Skateboarding Legend

HAYNES, MIKE
NFL Hall of Famer

HEGSETH, PETE
Army Veteran, Fox Nation Host,
New York Times Bestselling Author

HENDERSON, CHRIS
Guitarist for 3 Doors Down

HILTON, TYLER
Country Singer, Actor—
One Tree Hill

HOFFMAN, NICK
Singer, Songwriter, and Host of *Nick's Wild Ride*

HOGE, MERRIL
NFL Veteran Running Back, Former ESPN Analyst

HOUSHMANDZADEH, T. J.
NFL Veteran Wide Receiver

IACONELLI, MIKE
Professional Fisherman, Bassmaster Champion

IGGULDEN, CONN
Coauthor of *The Dangerous Book for Boys* Series

IRVIN, MICHAEL
NFL Hall of Fame Wide Receiver

ISLES, CARLIN
World's Fastest Rugby Player

JACKSON, HUE
NFL Head Coach and Founder of Stranger2Changer

JAMES, JOHN
United States Army Veteran, Apache Pilot

JENNINGS, STRUGGLE
Country Rapper

KANE, ALEXANDER
Actor and Producer

KELLY, JIM
NFL Hall of Fame Quarterback

KERREY, BOB
Medal of Honor Recipient, Former United States Senator, Nebraska

KEUILIAN, BEDROS
Founder of Fit Body Boot Camp

KHALIPA, JASON
World CrossFit Champion

KLAVAN, ANDREW
Edgar Award–Winning Author

KLEIN, BILL
Reality TV Star—*The Little Couple*

KOWAL, MARCUS
MMM Fighter, Founder of Liam's Life Foundation

LEA, BRAD
Founder and CEO of LightSpeed VT

LINDELL, MIKE
Founder of My Pillow

LIVELY, TRAVIS
Navy SEAL Veteran, Screenwriter

LOHMAN, AARON
Retired NYPD Sergeant

LOTT, RONNIE
NFL Hall of Fame Defensive Back

LUTTRELL, MARCUS
Navy SEAL Veteran and *New York Times* Bestselling Author of *Lone Survivor*

MANNING, DREW
Creator of *Fit2Fat2Fit*

MANGOLD, NICK
NFL Veteran, Entrepreneur

MARION, JOEL
Entrepreneur, Bestselling Author, Podcaster

MARSH, I. V.
Lead Pastor of BComing.Church

MARTIN, CURTIS
Health and Wellness Coach

MARTINI, MAX
Hollywood Actor—*Saving Private Ryan, Pacific Rim*

MATSON, SEAN
Navy SEAL, CEO of MATBOCK, CEO of CardoMax, CEO of Decon Products

MCDERMOTT, DEAN
Actor—*Open Range*

MCHALE, JOEL
Actor, Comedian—*The Soup*

MCNAMARA, PAT
Retired Delta Force Operator and Founder of TMACS Inc

MELTZER, BRAD
New York Times Bestselling Author

MELTZER, DAVID
Cofounder of Sports 1 Marketing

MEYER, DAKOTA
United States Marine, Medal of Honor Recipient

MICHLER, RYAN
Host of the *Order of Man* Podcast

MORELLI, MICHAEL
Personal Trainer, Founder of Morellifit

MULLER, MICHAEL
Award-winning Professional Photographer

MYLETT, ED
Entrepreneur Top 50 Wealthiest Under 50

NELSON, SHAWN
Founder and CEO of LuvSac

NICHOLS, JEFF
Navy SEAL Veteran

NORTON, CHRIS
Keynote Speaker, Author of *The Seven Longest Yards*

O'NEIL, TITUS
WWE Superstar

ORTIZ, TITO
UFC Hall of Fame Fighter

OSMAN, CHRIS
United States Marine and Navy SEAL Veteran

PAGE, BUBBA
Entrepreneur and Investor

PALMER, CARSON
Heisman Trophy Winner and #1 Overall NFL Draft Pick in 2003

PALMER, JORDAN
NFL Veteran Quarterback

PATTERSON, CHRIS
Entrepreneur, Owner of Interchanges

PATTERSON, ROSS
Actor, Producer, Host of *Drinkin' Bros* Podcast

PAVLIK, KELLY
Former Boxing WBO, WBC, Lineal Middleweight Champion

PEARLMAN, OZ
Mentalist, Emmy Award Winner, *America's Got Talent* Finalist

PERKINS, BILL
Professional Poker Player, Author

PHILLIPS, RICHARD
Merchant Mariner Captured by Somali Pirates

POMPEO, MIKE
Former United States Secretary of State

POWELL, CHRIS
Host of *Extreme Weight Loss, New York Times* Bestselling Author

PRATHER, CHAD
Host of *The Chad Prather Show*

RASO, DOM
Navy SEAL Team Six Veteran

REDMAN, JASON
Navy SEAL, Purple Heart Recipient, and *New York Times* Bestselling Author of *The Trident*

REES, ERIK
Founder of Team NEGU and the Jessie Rees Foundation

REID, SCOTT
Two-Time Britain's Strongest Man

REINFELD, KILAY
Partner and President of Paradigm Sports Management

RIORDAN, NEIL
PhD, Applied Stem Cell Research

RITLAND, MIKE
Navy SEAL Veteran and *New York Times* Bestselling Author of *Trident K-9 Warriors*

ROLOFF, MATT
Reality TV Star—*Little People, Big World*

ROSENBERG, SID
Host of *Bernie and Sid in the Morning on WABC*

RUTHERFORD, DAVID
Navy SEAL Veteran

RUTLEDGE, MICHAEL
Nightstalker Pilot and Navy SEAL Veteran

SALZHAUER, MICHAEL
Plastic Surgeon Known As Dr. Miami

SANTILLO, CHRIS
Author of *Resilience Parenting*

SAPAULA, MATT
United States Marine, Money Smart Guy

SAWYER, CRAIG
Navy SEAL Veteran, Founder of Vets For Child Rescue (V4CR)

SCHAUB, BRENDAN
UFC Fighter, Podcaster, and Stand-up Comedian

SCHECHTERLE, JASON
Motivational Speaker and Subject of *Burning Shield*

SHELTON, TRENT
Founder of Christian-based Organization RehabTime

SHOCKEY, JIM
Outfitter, Author, Host of *Jim Shockey's The Professionals* and *Uncharted*

SIMS, STEVE
Author, Speaker, Coach, Known as the Real-life Wizard of Oz

SINGERMAN, AARON
Bodybuilder, CEO of REDCON1

SLIWA, CURTIS
Founder of the Guardian Angels

SNOW, ERIC
Founder of the Watch D.O.G.S.

STEWMAN, RYAN
The Hardcore Closer

STOCKMAN, SHAWN
Singer, Songwriter, Boyz II Men

STROESSER, JIM
Entrepreneur, CEO of Cali Strong

SUTTER, RYAN
Firefighter, First Winner of *The Bachelorette*

SYLVER, MARSHALL
Hypnotist, Magician

THOMAS, KENNY
The Dancing Dad

TIMMONS, JEFF
Singer, Songwriter, 98 Degrees

TIPPETT, ANDRE
NFL Hall of Fame Linebacker

TREJO, DANNY
Hollywood Actor and Restaurateur

TRUMP, ERIC
Executive Vice President of Trump Organization

UTSCH, JEFF
Navy SEALs Swimming Instructor

VARGAS, VINCENT "ROCCO"
Army Rangers Veteran and Hollywood Actor—*Mayans M.C., Range 15*

VAN ORDEN, DERRICK
Navy SEAL Veteran, Actor

VERA, ROBERT
Bestselling Author and Motivational Speaker

VINCENT, TROY
Executive Vice President of NFL Football Operations

WARNER, KURT
Super Bowl MVP and NFL Hall of Fame Quarterback

WATSON, BENJAMIN
NFL Veteran Tight End, Super Bowl Champion

WAYNE, COLIN
Founder and CEO of Redline Steel

WEATHERFORD, STEVE
NFL Veteran Punter, Super Bowl Champion, NFL's Fittest Man

WEAVER, JASON
Actor, Singer—*The Lion King*

WEST, ALLEN
Former Congressman, Army Lieutenant Colonel

WHALEN, SEAN
CEO and Founder of Lions Not Sheep

WHITE, DANA
UFC President

WILLIAMS, MATTHEW
Green Beret, Medal of Honor Recipient

WILLINK, JOCKO
Navy SEAL Veteran and *New York Times* Bestselling Author

WOLF, JOSH
Comedian

WOLF, ROBB
Research Biochemist, Health Expert, Author of *The Paleo Solution*

WOODSON, ROD
NFL Hall of Fame Defensive Back, Super Bowl Champion

WOODSON, DARREN
NFL Veteran Safety, Three-time Super Bowl Champion

About the Author

ALEC LACE, father of four, launched his popular podcast, *First Class Fatherhood*, in 2018, with a vision to change the narrative of fatherhood and family life. The show quickly became one of the top parenting podcasts in America, due to Alec's interviews with some of the most recognized fathers in the world from all different fields, including Dean Cain, Deion Sanders, Tony Hawk, and Dana White.

Because of the show's popularity, Alec was invited to be on the field for the Super Bowl LIII media day in 2019, to interview dads such as Tom Brady, Julian Edelman, and Bill Belichick.

Our nation's military heroes hold a special place in Alec's heart. He has interviewed legendary servicemen such as Navy SEALs Rob O'Neill and Marcus Luttrell, *Black Hawk Down* pilot Mike Durant, Benghazi survivor John Tiegen, and Medal of Honor recipients Ed Byers, Dakota Meyer, and Michael Thornton.

On June 16, 2019, Alec was interviewed live on *Fox & Friends* for Father's Day and has also appeared on several other top podcasts, including *Order of Man* and *Life of Dad*.

Alec does all of this while continuing to be a dedicated railroad mechanic, a position he has held for twenty years, and an Uber driver on weekends.